TRIUMPH HOUSE

Spiritual Reflections 2007

Edited by Annabel Cook & Michelle Afford

First published in Great Britain in 2006 by:
Triumph House
Remus House
Coltsfoot Drive
Peterborough
PE2 9JX
Telephone: 01733 898102
Website: www.forwardpress.co.uk

SB ISBN 1 84431 086 8

Foreword

This unique anthology offers an uplifting and contemplative assortment of expressions in verse, musing on the physical, spiritual and emotional world we live in. Featuring works that can be enjoyed by all lovers of poetry throughout the year, each page holds an inspirational gem.

As Triumph House editors we have meticulously selected these poems from an abundance of entries to compile an anthology to cherish and enjoy for years to come. The talent of the authors to craft the language and express themselves, combined with their intuitive view of life, create a series of enlightening compositions that have been a joy to work with.

Containing spiritually stimulating and thought-provoking words that will engage and charm, *Spiritual Reflections 2007* is a collection of enthralling poetry to accompany you throughout the year ahead.

Annabel Cook & Michelle Afford

Editors

Contents

The Poems

Orison

You are here beside me walking every step.
Never wearied of Your vigil throughout the hours I've slept.
You draw the salted sting of every tear I've wept.
When I falter You are strong -
Leading me back to the righteous path -
Whene'er I stray on the wrong.
The salve of my conscience - rolling the rock from the tomb,
Resurrecting my comatose soul.
Restoring its beauty and bloom.

When my voice becomes a whimper, when uncertainty shines thro'
You temper the core of my argument with your covenant of the truth.

The lattice for my vine as my fruits burst forth and grow,
There in the shadow of my grief -
A seneschal shepherd behoving the bellicose behemoth cease.
In my joy you laugh the loudest,
Of my achievements You are the proudest.
You prime me with your inspiration to fire my best of shots.
To patiently untie all knots,
Pick all locks and search for clues.
To be prepared to walk a mile in another's painful shoes.
Then to comprehend each dolour rather than abuse.

To give thanks is all I have to give -
Yet, is all You ask of me.
And willingly I gladly do -
This night on bended knee.

Philip J Mee

. . . But There Is A Way

Within the stillness of God's night when the body is at rest,
When the conscience grips the troubled mind and brings
the final test,
To whom is it we turn when we wish our cares to end?
It is God and God alone on whom our prayers depend.

He is the one above all others, who accepts our hidden fears.
We pray that He may understand our thoughts and these are
what He hears.
In the tangled web that rules our lives, problems seem to mount;
At times they seem to reach a point that is far too great to count.

We pray that He may understand and listen to our fears,
That He may calm our hearts and this is what He hears.
No answers are immediate, solutions are not plain.
The time will come. We must wait. Nothing is in vain.

When all the joy of life has gone and no meaning seems to stay,
It is then that God awaits our call. It is time for us to pray.
When there seems no sun to shine and birds no longer sing,
It is then we find the help we seek, that only God can bring.

Ronald Moore

Count Your Blessings

God is there for us every time we pray
Listening to our troubles, be it night or day
He understands our problems and knows just how we feel
When we take them to Him as we get down and kneel
But we shouldn't only do it when we are feeling sad
It is just as important to talk to Him when we're glad
Glad of all the good things that happen in our life
For somewhere in this world there is famine, war and strife
So thank the Lord up above for countries that are at peace
And pray for the less fortunate, hoping their wars will cease.

Diana Daley

Sleep In Peace

As I lie here in the night, Father,
Let my heart be still.
Let me be doing Thy will.
Help me to think what I have done today,
In what I have done and what I have had to say.
Forgive me for the work left undone,
Tomorrow is another day.
I pray for the sick and those in need,
Dear Father, send help with extra speed.
Help me love my fellow man,
To give help where I can.
And as my day draws to a close,
Let me be thinking of those,
Who in far-off countries live
Father guide them and give
Them everlasting peace.
For Yours is the glory in life and death,
Let me sleep, my God, let me rest.

Carol Bernadette Boneham

Runaway

Missing from home, out there on your own.
Give us a sign, or pick up the phone.
Whatever the reason that took you away.
Give us a chance to tell you today.
You're in our hearts and prayers every night.
We pray for your safety and hope you're alright.
Know that we love you, and always will.
Pick up the phone, or come home better still.
If you feel that the time is not right.
Come home when you can, or phone us tonight.
Then we will know that you're in good health.
Those words to us, mean much more than wealth.
If there are others who are also out there,
You too! have loved ones at home who care.

Audrey Walker

Memories Are Friends

If you are sat at home on your own
Just think of your memories as friends
Sit down and think of those happy days
It can cheer you up in so many ways
It can help you to relive the past

All those people from the past you knew
Think of your family, where you went and what you did
Those happy days, I am sure were many
Trips to the seaside by bus and by train
With tired, hungry children, then back home again.

Jam sandwiches and cold tea and picnics in the park
Stopping out all day until it gets dark
Bonfire nights were such a lark
With Catherine wheels
My favourites,
Sparklers, held in the hand
And the jumping cracker

The best memories to remember are
Watching the flames in the fire's embers
The kettle on the hob singing away
Water bubbling in the tank by the fire
Or perhaps cakes baking in the oven

The best thing of all I like to see
Is the toasting fork doing muffins for tea
Toasting your toes at the same time -
You see even a coal fire can be your friend

Audrey Allott

Untitled

Lord, how many times
Must I forgive my brother
When he sins against me
Seven times
Not seven, Peter, but seventy times seven

That's a lot, my Master
Shall we just say forever?
Jesus paid forever
For everyone He paid

What's that again, then Master
Is it something better?
The next world it will be
And Heaven, yes, my Saviour

With us, yes, God will be
No more night, only day
Forever God we'll see
Will we not sleep then, Master?

No more sickness
No more pain
No more death, we'll see
No more murder, rape and violence
Of these, we'll all be free

We'll be like the angels
Jesus said, 'My Son
Faithful love forever
With God we will be one
Amen
Jesus Christ
My prayer
God, my Saviour, *Amen.*

B Pail

Reclamation

If your life's been scarred by shameful indiscretion
That dark despondency in which you wallow
Makes you view each situation with suspicion
Because trust becomes a bitter pill to swallow

You may feel that life's no longer worth the living
Guilt and shame have torn your once-chaste world apart
And you see no way to realise redemption
For a deep despair pervades your languid heart

Your self-confidence may well have been depleted
But that doesn't mean it's totally destroyed
If you'll dare embrace three principles of spirit
You can then reclaim your life back from the void

Dare to love, and dare to trust, and dare to live life
If your self-inflicted ghosts, you'd exorcise
Dare to be the person that you know you can be
Unreservedly, and without compromise.

Ron Beaumont

The Warmth Of Your Smile

The warmth of your smile will leave a glow
With people you meet, wherever you go.
It costs you nothing to leave it there
And so much nicer than leaving a stare.
If you smile whatever you do
You'll find that folk give theirs back to you
The more you give it, the more you get
So give away loads and spread your net
To gather in a host of friends
And see how much joy your smile lends.

Stroma M Hammond

Coincidence?

So many times in life did I set out,
A brash, unswerving, confident young man:
My way clear-cut according to a plan
Untrammelled by anxiety or doubt.
But, time and time again, the unforeseen,
Deflecting my unwavering resolve,
Would lead to pathways destined to evolve
Fresh views of what might otherwise have been.
Such quirks of fate I never understood.
I ponder on them often even now.
Capricious chance? Perhaps: and yet, I vow
My heart suspects the friendly hand of God!
'Coincidence' some deem it. Well, not I,
More, 'angel's footsteps' presaging the way.

John M Beazley

Did You Laugh?

Did you laugh at their rough looks
Because being in a fight did not get them off the hook?
They were still thrown out of the place
Somewhere else and somebody, they would have to learn to hate.

Did you laugh at their rough looks?
At those people taking fright?
Running here, then running there
About what do they really care?

Did you laugh at their rough looks
As you laid them down to sleep?
Where would they all sleep tonight?
What pleasure do they get from having a fight?

Keith L Powell

An Idea Is Born

Dreamy clouds above the lake
Drifting, hopeful, taking shape
Wafting softly towards the sea
Thunder is rumbling ahead
Dreams have been set free
Oceans are bubbling red
Magma shooting high
A chaotic fountain
Burning the sky
Ambitions cry!
'To climb is exertion
But we must try!'
Waves whip my heels
As I battle towards the peak
Lightning strikes my fear
I grow weary on my feet
Drowning in the raindrops
I hold on so I don't slip
I cut my hands on jagged rocks
I nearly lose my grip
Blinded by the hail
Deafened by the wind
I realise I might just fail
And wonder *why did I begin?*
Determined, I proceed
Though not at a great speed
All that really matters
Is progression towards the peak
So I will keep on climbing
And one day I will succeed . . .

The idea was easy
The planning was hard
The first step seemed impossible
And the middle fell apart
I pieced it back together
The 'finish' is still far away
But if I never give up
I'll reach my goal one day.

Natasha Brand

Worship Song

You are my treasure,
Love You, Lord, forever,
Good Shepherd and King,
Your praises I'll sing!

You are my Saviour,
You are my friend,
You've promised to be with me
Right to the end.

I lay down my burdens
Here at Your feet,
Things that would stop me
From yielding to You.

I bow down and worship,
Give You the best of me -
My talents, time and energy,
I lay before Your throne.

Cathy Mearman

Who Dreams It Not

A dream of dreams,
Styled to suit,
To hope to be,
Not be what will,
To cope better,
Than we would,
Without a say
From any other,
To give more than to get,
Eating all that's best,
Doing more good than we can,
Saving more than we could,
Helping out all over,
Far beyond our reach.

Rachel Taylor

At Easter Time

Oh! Make my life, Lord Jesus
As Thy robe without a seam.
A living true example
Of Your vision. Perfect dream.
May my arms cling to Your beauty
As Your garment, from Your neck.
Let my soul remain unbroken
Should it strive within a wreck.
Make me give loving kindness
As You did in the days of yore
Until Your loving arms have found me
Holy, seamless, evermore.
Leaving those Temple Courts
The little band, crossing the Cedron to Gethsemane,
There meeting Judas with the silvered hand -
One who had forgotten Galilee.
His broken heart, His agony, His trial,
Coupled up with Peter's great denial
The road to Calvary brought sorrow, all the way,
Leaving those Temple Courts,
To change our night to day.
If I could pray with my head crowned with thorn,
Blood on my face, garments all torn,
If I could walk on the tempestuous sea,
Tell weary fishermen where they should be
I should be like Him.
If I could give all my purse to the poor
Speak to the multitudes on every shore.

If I could heal the blind and the lame,
Call every living thing by its name
I should be like Him,
Oh! When He comes riding high on the clouds,
Lifting me up from the great trembling crowds
Keeping His promises, making it loud,
I shall be like Him, and I shall see Him,
As He is!

Elsie Horrocks

God Lives On The Washing Line

A pair of bootees.
A weathered old shirt.
A row of toe-holed socks.

A flannelette nightie.
A ripped pair of jeans.
A rugby shirt that's had too many knocks.

Lacy underwear.
Too short a shirt.
A trio of calico frocks.

Saggy jogging bottoms.
Pristine shirts.
Ties that really do shock.

Pegs at the ready.
Is that a black cloud?
Racing against the clock.

The hated school uniform.
The Led Zeppelin T-shirt.
The evening dress - so elegant and fine.

The Barbie-pink pyjamas.
Teddy - sparkling and clean.
Survived his encounter with red wine.

A bright orange scarf?
A hideous red sweatshirt?
Can't remember those being mine.

Numerous vests.
Vast numbers of tights.
Endless towels - eight - no, nine.

Time for a cuppa,
And to count my blessings.
Yes, God lives on the washing line.

Anne Marie Latham

A Little Song

(A joyful song, a thankful song: a welcome little song)

Lilting voices singing
In pleasing harmony
Telling all who listen
That love now holds the key:
Lilting voices greeting
Emmanuel.

Saying, 'I love You,
Oh how I love You,
New days are filled with peacefulness
Given, dear Lord, by You.'

A joyful song, a thankful song: a welcome little song.

Loving words are winging
Into God's Heaven blue:
Thankful words are telling
That life is now brand new:
Loving words all praising
Emmanuel.

Saying, 'I thank You,
Oh how I thank You,
New hope shines brightly day and night
Given, dear Lord, by You.'

Violet M Corlett

Think Of Me . . .

Think of me when you go to sleep,
Innermost thoughts, only you can keep.
In this world of fantasy and fun,
A whole new episode of your life has just begun.

Think of me when you sleep tonight,
When you close your eyes shut tight.
Could you make my body a 'temple'?
Worship me from night till morn.

Amanda Simpson-Cleghorn

To See A Sunset At Early Dawn

To see a sky ablaze with God's creation,
To see the birds fly to and fro;
Building their nests,
For the babies to come.

They come into a world,
That was made for them;
The little birds fly to and fro,
Oblivious of what goes on below.

The sound of war,
This is a world of peace,
God gave it all our fellow men;
What happened to them in-between?

God's gift of love is all around,
For all to grasp and have each day;
Let's not distress us with war and wounds;
Let's pray for a land of peace,

Where love cannot fail if all is well,
And we all can again
See the beauty that is free for all;
And see the sun set in a worldly glow.

Mabel Houseman

Last Night

Lord, while I was asleep last night
Someone painted the streets white
A beautiful deep colour of white
As if it were a fluffy blanket

It's like everything has been obliterated
For You, Lord, that must be what You see
A sea of white undulating over the land
I bet it looks wonderful from where You sit

Last night.

Carole A Cleverdon

This World

The day is filled with voids
The morrow brings sorrow
Nothing gives hope
To this tired heart
This heart so full of hate
This same heart so selfish
Filling me with shame
My world is such a mess!

Tears in my eyes
Tears in my blood
This joy overwhelms me
This joy overflows
I, a sinner, know You!
I, a sinner
Called by Christ

In the darkness I see You
Ever beside me
In this madness perceive You
Mending this heart
Your will is for us
Your love gives me peace

One heart unlike mine
Helps me hope
One day to be like You
And as I hope, I see
This heart growing in love
This heart growing in strength.

Emmanuel Ntezeyombi

Friends

Rebecca and Carole
This one's for you
As each day arrives
You get me through

You're both good friends
With hearts big and warm
Your kindness and caring
See me through the storm

Mistakes and bad comments
Yes, I've made my share
But nasty to people?
I wouldn't harm a hair!

You two are rocks
Your advice is so sound
I'd just crack completely
Without you around

You're as old as the hills!
Just a joke, that it be
Don't be offended
You look young, just like me!

Counting the calories
Won't help the fat
In my opinion
You've both none of that!

I'll end here for now
Before I dig me a hole
But, my dears, you're the best!
Please continue this role.

Adam Poole

Echoes Of Childhood

As I walked past this church
Unconventional in its simplicity
I heard the same words
The same tune, week after week
As if by providence
It was for me to learn
To learn untaught
Except by my own ears
Their ability to listen and grasp
They were my best teachers -
My ears

Soon I hummed the tune
The words fell into place
Proudly I felt part of the congregation
Albeit from the outside
A young girl - no match
For the generation inside

The words they went:
'O sing blazes
O sing blazes
O sing blazes to God most high
For His goodness and compassion
For His goodness and compassion
O sing blazes, O sing blazes
O sing blazes to God most high'

This I had learnt by myself
A sense of achievement I felt
An uplifting tune
My special companion

I sang through my early teens
To early adulthood
Numerous others there were
But, 'O sing blazes'!
It was jolly and simple

As a young mum
I still sang, 'O sing blazes'

Then one day it clicked
I should be singing
'O sing *praises*
To God most high
For His goodness and compassion . . .'

What a laugh!
God must have been having a giggle
All those years

Ellen Rollings

Remember Youth

Here's to our youth,
The days we spent in the sun.
Those special days out,
With a close loved one.
Those days on the beaches,
Where our spirits ran free,
To the days in front of the fire,
Or singing around the Christmas tree.
Remember kicking a ball?
Or just dressing a doll?
Just sitting around talking,
Watching the leaves fall?
Our youth is so precious,
We should cherish it well,
Because before we know it,
We're all grown up.
Life is full of problems and mistrust.
So keep youth in your heart
And your memories near,
And you'll always be young
No matter how old you are.

Donna Salisbury

Paula

(To Janet and Fred)

When you hear a blackbird sing,
Perched high, or on the wing.
Quiet thoughts of comfort
These joyful songs will bring.
The love for birds, and past
Company of one so dear,
Will bring you close together
And eliminate the fear.
A peaceful time observing,
Nature's wondrous sights.
Memories of time spent watching
White owls and red kites.
A drive to Pegwell Bay
On a cold winter's day.
Hats, coats and binoculars
To the nature reserve -
Coastal birds are plentiful
And delightful to observe.
As you watch and listen,
I know that you will find,
Paula, very close to you,
Her love forever held -
Safely in your mind.

Janey Wiggins

Relax And Chill

God'll come to you, relax and chill
no need to rush around, relax, be still
you can break records, with your dedication
empty vessels will be filled, relaxing meditation
knock off the mind, and it's open, the door
relax and chill, because less is more
happiness (the butterfly), can land if you are still
God'll come to you, relax and chill.

Mark Musgrave

Motion

Every sunset captures that feeling.
The sinking, the longing, the loving,
the needing.

Beauty of innocence sails me to sleep.
From a life that is shallow,
to a love that is deep.

And in my darkest minute,
I can hear her breathing.
Louder grows the silence,
as her eyes begin the healing.

But whispers follow as I fall at your grace,
for this love surrounds me.
At last I am safe . . .

Owais Kazmi

Life After Death

We were brought
Together by
Deaths, the children
And friends,
Put their hands
Together to bring
Life to mine,
Before the end of time,
To seek many adventures,
And to live my life
Again, may their
Ventures not be in vain.

B Brown

Don't Be Afraid Of Mr Freud

Why call it 'talking to yourself'?
Why not 'expressing thoughts aloud'?
Why let them question mental health,
Make you ashamed and then feel proud?

How can you know just what you think
Until you hear the things you say?
When standing at the kitchen sink
It is aloud I often pray.

For atheists there is no God.
They'd call it talking to myself.
They'd definitely call me odd
And call in question mental health.

Although this does not worry me,
It makes me just a bit annoyed
And when alone, I feel quite free
To talk aloud to Mr Freud!

E Bright-Butler

Confession

Bless me, Father, for I have sinned.
I have met in the mirror
My guests gathering on the dark blue road.

Each has said one thing and thought another.
Each has said one thing and meant another.
Each has said nothing and thought nothing
And thought nothing and been nothing.
Each has bitten through a day and a dream.
Each, in a second, has made a world disappear.

Bless me, Father, for I have sinned,
It has been a second and many guests
Since my last confession.

David R Morgan

A Life Full Of Hope

(Dedicated to Emma Hirt)

Shimmering hope wields illumination,
Manoeuvres my soul towards Your great heart,
Of fulfilling dreams: wishing hope to start
The luminescence of imagination,
Of illuminating love's communion,
The fullness of life hereafter: apart,
The performance of hymns, lifting a start,
A Bible of fullness, determination,
My soul's willingness to be hopeful:
To make life alluringly right, to cope,
Fluorescence all around, fighting the lull
Of the past, dark frequently, into Hope:
Turning the spotlight towards prayer, new life,
Shadows burn and turn around a full life.

Edmund Saint George Mooney

This New Day

Please let this new day
be a new start,
let only loving thoughts flow from my heart.

Let all I may aim for,
be for everyone's good,
may I be mindful, of all that I should.

Let me keep *Jesus* close in my heart.
    Yes, please let this new day,
    be a new start.

Jacqueline Claire Davies

A Tie-Dyed Sky

Springtime sky, tie-dyed in multi-tonal hues;
Turquoise, azure, dazzling cerulean blues.
Snow-white clouds create a whimsical collage;
Fabricates the winsome semblance of mirage.

Down on earthly plane, sweet miracles occur.
Golden buttercup becomes a bold voyeur,
Bravely peeping through the verdant undergrowth,
Seeking out a floral soulmate to plight his troth.

Songbirds serenade grey squirrels in the park,
From the early light of dawn till dusky dark.
Dozy dormice stretch their tiny, stiffened limbs,
Blinking in the sunlight, hoping brightness dims.

Gleeful sounds of laughter fill the vernal air;
Children playing, running, dancing ev'rywhere.
Apathy has lifted; springtime brings a smile.
Happiness is here, if only for a while.

Wendy Wilson

His Golden Glow

Lovely days of yesteryear that blossom in my mind
are watered by the memories of a love that once was mine,
She's in the garden of my heart renewed in every way
warmed by her sweet love each and every day,
The sweetest little spring flower that came into my life,
the darling, sweet primrose, the name of my darling wife,
Who long ago went home to rest; there's a little garden
where the Lord takes care of all who go to Him
in a holy place that's always free from sin.
The Great One took my sweet love away because He loved her so,
And now she blossoms in the warmth of the Great One's
golden glow.

V N King

He Who Lives Within Me

In this world and within my human state
I am nothing and I am worthless
But in God I am everything and I am worthy
To be in the presence of God.

I may have everything I need that this world offers me
But without God I have nothing.
I am poor,

I may have nothing within that this world offers me
But *if* I have God within my life, I have everything I need,
I am rich.

I may not be successful within this world,
I'm not looking for false success.

I am successful in God.
He who lives within me (God) is much, much *greater*
Than the one (Satan) that roams the world.

C J Walls

Candle Glow

We have just one chance to make our mark
To light a candle in the dark
To show the way forward into the light
Even through the darkest night
To be thankful for each and every new day
And to face with courage what comes our way
There'll be laughter and tears, hopes and fears
To share with those that we hold dear
I pray that my candle burns bright and strong
To help light your way when the road seems long
And when my life on Earth is through
I'll never be far away from you
If you light your candle and let it shine
And glow forever alongside mine

P Booker

The Path Of Life

Keep on searching for your peace and always look for love
Remember that life is a journey that is over far too quickly

Measure each success from within, without pride or arrogance
Make sure you leave only memories and joy, not hate or regret

Help those around you feel safe and protected
Because fear is our main predator which can consume us

Delight in each passing sunrise; each plaintive birdsong
Never forget to wonder and ask the questions of time

In all your travels, greet others with understanding and compassion
Without presuming of their attitude and state of mind

At all times believe that the only person you have to prove
Anything to is yourself and your God,
And He will understand, whatever the result.

Smile at those sent to tempt or hinder you,
As they have lost their way
Resolve to assist them to regain the path to their peace

Do not waste energy on wanting things you do not have
Always be calm and at peace, looking for joy in all that surrounds you

For every moment in time be truthful to your own identity
Do not paint a façade that belongs to another,
As you will be found out

Continue on this path without deviation
And falter, with your eyes straight ahead
And then be assured the final step will be the greatest of all.

Sam Kelly

Nan, You are . . .

Nan, you are the first snowdrop in spring,
You are a beautiful butterfly that has spread its wings,
You are the first bird that sings,
You are so many wonderful things.

Nan, you are the smell of a delicate rose,
You are the warmth of woolly socks on cold toes,
You are a mountain covered with snow,
You are the love that no one else knows.

Nan, you are the colours of the rainbow,
You are the first ray of light to show,
You are a present tied with a big bow,
You are the kindest person I know.

Nan, you are a tall oak tree,
You are the rush of the sea,
You are a fuzzy bumblebee,
You mean so much to me.

Nan, you are a freshly baked cake,
You are a strawberry milkshake,
You are a special keepsake,
You are this life we can make.

Nan, you are a bright shining star,
You will always be there, wherever you are,
Even when we are apart,
Nan, you are forever in my heart.

Dawn Powell

Restored In Christ

Christened as a baby
Though I didn't understand
The wonders of creation
Designed by God's own hand
I grew through the Church
Through all my childhood years
Though I never knew the Lord
Who comforts us
And wipes away our tears

I gave my life to Jesus
Redeemed and then baptised
Living for the Lord
I was marked, mocked and despised
My baptism should have mattered
At least, I thought it did
Yet I lost sight of this
And so I then backslid

I was seventeen, a Christian
Spirit-filled and led
I let my faith grow colder
And my fire for God went dead
Cos living as a Christian
Was inconvenient for me
I'd forgotten about the price He paid
To truly set me free

It's not easy to follow a moral code
That society rejects today
Thank God, He brought me to my senses
Back into the narrow way
And now I want to know Him more
Each and every day
We do this through our Bible, through worship
And when we pray

It is hard to live our faith
By the Christian code today
Personal morality, fidelity and chastity
Is the Christian way
Trusting God knows best
Anointed and sealed by God
I'm justified and blessed

Immorality and sin are offences against our Lord
So we must be standing firm
In love and one accord
And I say with firm conviction
I'm living for You
Lord!

Mark Walker

The Wonder

Oh, tiny bird, how did you know
Who gave you skill so rare
To make a warm and fragile nest
With so much love and care?

You have no hands or fingers neat
To shape the mossy wall,
Or weave the lichen with sheep's wool
While singing mates recall.

A hundred grey down feathers line
This precious home for chicks,
Whose shape is reinforced about
With little bits of sticks.

I saw a nest built just like yours
On Ballinabearna's Hill,
And though it's sixty years ago
The wonder's with me still.

Mary Lefebvre

Don't Be Frightened

(Written for my dad on 10/11/01 when the prognosis for his cancer was very bad.
He's still fighting . . . and winning)

What's that noise, Mum?
Please, turn on the light,
I can't stand the thought
Of movements in the night . . .
What's that shadow
Flickering on the wall?
I'm watching the open doorway
But there's nothing there at all . . .
There might be someone waiting
At the very top of the stairs
Look, I see him moving!
Oh no, it's just a chair . . .
I must check my wardrobe
Well, you know, just in case
(A thousand hairy monsters
Could fit in that huge space . . .)

Don't be afraid of the dark, my dear,
Nor of things you can't explain,
When you blow away the shadows
Only light and love remain.
Don't worry about what you cannot see,
These demons in your head,
I'm here to switch the lights on,
Hold your hand, kiss your cheek, and tuck you back in bed . . .

Michele Amos

Ever Hopeful

Sometimes you may abandon your dreams,
But don't ever abandon your hopes!
They will get you thro' the darkest hour,
When you feel you are 'on the ropes'.

We can only live in our consciousness,
But each day, we start anew.
Not knowing, what's round the corner,
Or where life will take us to!

It's *hope* that keeps us all going,
Our dreams, we can change, on the way!
Life, is mostly a compromise,
Hope, gets us through each new day!

Opportunity, chance, or circumstance,
Can alter our lives, in a flash,
But never relinquish your heartfelt hopes,
Just because a dream took a crash!

I am eighty years of age, but I still
Have things I would love to do!
Loss of mobility may shake my dreams,
But *hope,* makes me feel they'll come true!

E M Eagle

The Blessing

I am in a cloud, a mist
of love and peace,
not in my troubled mind, but in my heart.
I hear the music though there is no sound,
I am nurtured in life's daily round
by faith and peace, but also
know that peace surrounds,
it's from out there and meets in here;
and I know I am found,
I am found, I am found.

Sheila O'Hara

Earth Angels

Angels are not only in Heaven,
Many are here on our Earth,
They do thoughtful things, when we are sad,
So oblivious of their worth . . .

The friends who are always there,
Who will never let you down;
They will help you out, whate'er the task,
Without so much as a frown . . .

People who we meet, just once,
Along life's busy way;
They take the time, to say 'Hello'
And brighten up your day . . .

These deeds may seem so small,
To some - who have so many things;
But to the ones, who haven't much in life,
They can mean everything . . .

Earth angels aren't aware,
How they can fill a lonely part
Of life, when one is left alone,
To help mend a broken heart . . .

But then angels, are made in Heaven,
They bring love with them, from birth,
To spread around - to whom they meet,
And to take away each hurt . . .

So, if you get to meet one,
Please tell them of their worth;
And try to give them in return,
Love - entwined - with mirth . . .

Janet Starkey

What Price Democracy?

The way to democracy
Is not an easy one
The ancient Greeks discovered that
When first they tried it on
Rights carry responsibilities
Which some are loath to claim
Freedom of speech, freedom of choice
Should still be there for everyone.
Another nail in the coffin of freedom
Was driven home today
No smoking, no eating, no drinking
Too unhealthy to receive healthcare
Too outspoken to speak your mind
The reasoning appears to be
It will cost the government money
Or offend some jealous groups
I do not smoke or hunt
But surely those who do
Have a right to their decisions
To live their lives the way
They choose to do
The money we give our country
Should benefit all not just a few
To live a lawful, peaceful life
Democracy should mean
Freedom for the individual
Whilst remembering other people
Have lives they cherish too

B Williams

I Have A Dream

The path ahead stares at me
Do I choose the road less travelled
Or do I choose the short cuts?
There's so much I want
There's so much to achieve
I'm energised
I'm anxious and excited
I anticipate this journey
The path that leads somewhere
The path that leads to other paths
My path ahead lies in front of me
There're so many expectations
I'm looking forward to these first steps
Steps that will turn into a million miles
I'll be miles away
I can't wait to take this first step
I'll be going to places
I'll be seeing new spaces and places
Traces of where I was will be left behind
I'll be on the move
This is my dream
'I have a dream'
Time is ticking fast
Life is in the fast lane
I'm ready to live this dream
This dream I've had for a long time
This dream that haunted me every night
A dream that spoke to me
It made me listen to its meaning
I'm dreamy if for the longest time
This is now, because I'm alive
'I have a dream'.

Matome Mahasha

A Matter Of Taste

Through it all the rotting, crooked
Bridge has seen it all, it was sturdy
Once upon a time, but the stone
Supports are cracked. And then
One day it might fall down like
The Great Wall of China.
Anyway, it's a matter of taste
She was like that, like the early
Morning sun. She looked fresh as
The early morning dew.
I think she was made to just stand here.
A camera couldn't catch a more
Beautiful picture. A matter of taste
That she shared with the morning sun.
The wild pondlife lifted their eyes
To watch her, then carried on with their
Morning chores. A matter of taste
You might say, for the dawn of the day.
A matter of taste that one day the old
Bridge will fall down. And there'll be
No camera to catch the beautiful happening
So there she is, smelling of perfume,
Spreading over the pond, and her hand reaching
To her eyes to hide the glare of the sun.
And with a matter of taste, I'll be with her soon,
Like the old bridge, it's a matter of taste.

David Rosser

Remembrance Sunday

The ardent young pacifist, striving after peace,
Assumed that Christians joined him as he struggled in the search.
So on Remembrance Sunday, as he watched the British Legion
With their band and their banner on their way to church,
He fiercely protested. The scene that he saw
Meant the church and the Christians glorified war.

The preacher was old, and remembered the shambles
Of total war, and impressions made.
In fighting the horrors of Hitler's aggression
Men said, 'We are fighting a Christian crusade.'
But he could not connect such a self-righteous aim
With the methods employed to accomplish the same.

Now some of those present remembered their loved ones
Lost when they perished in various wars;
And some could relive the heroic self-sacrifice
Offered by those who were fighting a cause.
The preacher wrestled much in prayer to sort these matters out;
And asked the Lord to tell us what He thought it all about.

'I don't take sides in nations' wars by methods that you mention,
Nor sit advising generals who pay Me no attention;
For good and evil fight not so . . . your wars are not the whole.
My battleground is cosmic . . . and involves the human soul.

Yet you do well to recollect the horror and the blame,
For I was in the suffering, and I was in the shame.
But I'm against the cause of war: the hatred and the greed.
Why don't you go for those with Me, where'er you see the need?
It's love and sacrifice you want, not guns; and what is more:
The comradeship, endurance and the discipline of war.'

Simon Peterson

The Joy Of Family

For those of us endowed with family,
We share good fortune many others lack,
And we must recognise to what degree
We benefit, secure in our own pack.
We've access to so many things in life,
Companionship and love together come,
Support for one another, both in strife
As well as joy, for everyone's a chum!
We vent at one another, even fight;
How wonderful it is to let off steam!
No bottling up, no matter who is right,
For family means working as a team.
We're blessed to have such shared dependency
As we enjoy within our family.

Christopher Head

My Toothless Wonder

He is my toothless wonder, my friend of many years.
I can tell that he is happy by the toothless grin he wears.
I have tried to give him nibbles but he finds them hard to eat,
For, alas, he cannot crunch them, can only suck soft meat.
I sort of understand him for my teeth are going too,
I have a denture that is awkward but it does help me to chew.
He has always been a handsome chap even with no teeth
And just one eye.
He is flawless, he is faithful, his perfection is no lie.
I see him with the eyes of love, 'tis the way God looks at me.
I have prayed to see as God does, for 'tis the nicest way to see.
Indeed!

Rosie Hues

Stand

Stand with one purpose by telling the good news fearlessly
Stand firm, be patient, let nothing move you
Stand upright, the Risen Christ is in you
Stand firm in your saving grace
Stand firm in joys and sorrows
Stand firm on the hilltops and in the valleys
Stand against unjust persecution and opposition
Stand against modern trends in society
Stand on what you believe
Stand mighty against world view in speech and deeds
Stand amazed at your success
Stand firm by growing in faith and peace
Stand firm by following God's power and life's purposes
God takes His stand in all your circumstances
The Earth trembles and stands silently before the Lord
Above all, stand firm by surrendering to the Trinity.

Nicole Palan

Thought

Limitless journeys by stepping outside an unknown boundary
No predetermined infinity
Dependence no more on the perceived norm
Discovery of thought, pulsing in a conscious freedom
Emerging from a vague pulse to a main artery in the heart
                                            of creativity
Can thought ever complete the wholeness in soul?
Suppressing ever a featherlite thought
Not running with it and never knowing the outcome
Taking an initiative to strip the sometimes-numbing security
Preserved memory can dominate extended thought
Thought - now spiralling into invisible - merging into a
                                            new permanence
Uncoiling the inward unknown silence of thought
To have thought exhumed - have courage
A new thought!

Hilary Jean Clark

The Best Things In Life Are Free

If only we could realise,
        the best things in life are free,

We would have grasped the meaning
        of a true philosophy.

You cannot buy a contented mind
        or peace within the heart.

A conscience clear, or friends most dear,
        these are all a part of . . .

What must be earned as day by day
        we travel along life's road,

To do a kindness, give a smile
        or help to share a load.

We are all given the chances
        as we journey along life's way,

To do our best with what we are given
        every single day.

Edna Rudge

Untitled

God's spirit breathes upon me
Peace caresses my skin
Then seeps deeply beneath
Soothing tired nerves -
Sleepiness begins

Sweet peace gently descending
Its warmth like a blanket on my soul
I'm carried in its arms to my dreams
Kissed, kept secure in the Holy Ghost

Isabel Taylor

A Life In Seasons

In the springtime of my life, when I was young and foolish
all was new and experiences were different and varied.
As I grew, attitudes changed, so did ideas and early adult years
gave way to relationships and family values.
But summer didn't come then . . .

The winter came instead when unsteady half-truths
found their way into everyday life, mistrust ruled the roost
after twilight phone calls attempted to hurt and enrage.
That winter lasted for almost twenty years even after the absence
of the cold ice and snow.
Still the summer didn't come . . .

In my autumn I stripped off the old and clothed myself
with temporary dress, quiet thoughts on how life had changed
and where to go from here?
Ruminations on feelings came into play whereas previous attitudes
left no room and changing lifestyles helped to find what
was really important.
And only then did the summer finally come . . .

Summer is a quiet seat in your own back garden
where warm air entices you to breathe deeply.
Summer is knowing you're in the right when a wrong is done
but choosing not to press the matter home.
Summer is finding out about yourself, realising you are a nice person
after all, underneath all the winter snow, the autumn leaves
and the foolishness of spring.
Summer is allowing people to be who they are, always in the hope
that one day soon they will 'get it' and revel in 'it'.

Like a warm blanket that you pass on to a loved one
because they are foolish, or hurting, or reflecting.
And like spring, autumn and winter
summer is always on its way.

Sue Lane

There Was This Girl . . .

There was this girl, she was not in any way complete,
She found life hard, hard to stand on her own two feet.

Wandering aimlessly, with little meaning in her pointless life,
Her days became endlessly filled with sadness and strife.

On a downwards spiral, she hit the floor,
Trying to take her own life, was there any point anymore?

She started to go to church, try and turn her life to good,
Unsure what to believe, not sure if she should.

Then one day she finally knew, she had belief in Him above,
It was time to learn new things, to show the Lord her love.

As she reads the gospel, it fills her once sad heart and mind,
She's finally found the right path, the path she was meant to find.

So for forgiveness, joy and guidance, she begins to pray,
She spoke to the Lord, and in return He did say.

'I've been with you each step of the way, My child, without a doubt,
I saw your every move, when you made mistakes My heart did cry out.

But now you see you can change your life, and bring things new,
You are My child, be faithful to Me and I will look out for you.'

She can see hope in her life, more and more each day,
The Lord is there as her friend, in each and every way.

I'll keep the Lord, keep Him in my heart for evermore,
Thank you, Lord, for finding me, and opening this new door.

So now that person she used to be, that person has gone,
That 'she' is called Caroline, her journey has just begun.

Caroline Elizabeth Duffy

Bethlehem

Bethlehem Ephrath, land in Judea,
Fear not God's wrath, for from His idea,
A leader will come, from David's line,
From you, Bethlehem, a man, yet divine.

Like a shepherd caring for His lost sheep,
This ruler will care for His people.
And also will comfort those who do weep.
Each one will be a disciple.

God's glorious and powerful name
Will bring all this to holy fruition.
Jesus, the Messiah, is the divine,
Whose fame will turn doubt to recognition.

This man will bring love and peace
To those who believe in Him.
Through Him, all wars will cease.
At His birth, the seraphim
And angels who sit on high,
In the high realms with God above,
Will sing from out of the sky,
'Hark! For the King and His love!'

You, Bethlehem, are the one.
From out of you will come
A shepherd for my people, Israel.
The Christ whose love will never fail.

Christine M Wilkinson

Reborn Again

Reborn again, He said to me
Clean and fresh

For life in eternity
I thought that I had lost you

But I find my love
When I look above
So Heaven is eternal love
Fresh and new with love from above

So I say to you 'Happy Easter'
With love I send to you
From Heaven on Earth up above.

So I close my eyes and pray to Thee

Thank Thee, Lord
For loving me.

Debbie Storey

My Friend Edith

There is a lovely lady
Who is so gentle and kind
She will listen to your troubles
If you have some on your mind.

Edith makes you very welcome
Any time of day
It is very nice to see her
To pass an hour away.

She lives in a quaint old cottage
Somewhere in the Peak
A lovely little village
Not very far from Leek.

May Ward

Countryside Impressions

(Ps 104:24)

Dreamers dream of reaping
A great harvest;
But only the realists
Plough and sow.

A skilled ploughman
Cuts straight furrows,
And a discerning stockman
Rears a prize pedigree herd.

Better to be eating
Its steak than to be
Riding that bull.

A forester's song echoes in
The valley. His trained eye
Perceives nature such as
No city dweller can.

The flower show manifests
A spectacular profusion
Of colours. Each specimen
Declares the Creator's
Delicate and ingenious design.

Perfumiers' fragrances permeate
Every festive occasion.
They gather their ingredients
From nature's created bounties.

The Earth bears Your
Fingerprints, O Lord;
And reveals the marvels
Of Your handiwork.

Azariah Ephratah

Ascension Evening

A warm and pleasant evening
As we sat there on the ground
To sing a hymn of praises
By the ancient moorland mound.

There was a cuckoo calling
So soft and still the air
Our hearts were filled with wonder
We could feel God's presence there.

The moor became a lakeside
And His words were strong and sure
As when they were first spoken
All those many years before.

I listened to the gospel
Feeling, on that quiet moor
So near to Jesus teaching
By the Galilean shore.

Molly Rodgers

The Ruin

The ruins of a Buddhist monastery
Lie empty for hundreds of years
Filled for hundreds of years before this
By thousands of faceless men
In ages long forgotten
In lands no one has heard of
Lord, we are all so small.

William Ballantine

The Black Hole - A Prayer For The World

In this brave new world of 2006
The human race is led to believe
That somewhere out there
Way beyond our control
Lies an unknown factor - an enormous black hole.

As we become more accustomed to what science reveals
Our minds cannot grasp the truth of it all
Questions need answering but who can tell
Which mighty power could create such a space?

Perhaps it would be a convenient place
To drop in the sins of the human race?

Put in the hunger of those without food
The agony of victims suffering from AIDS
The abuse of young children and of those very old
In homes where love seems as rare as pure gold.

Throw in the discomfort of the homeless and cold
Their beds made of stone in the city so grim
Covers made tight with cardboard and string
Drop in the guilt of those who snatch babies
From the enfolding warmth of a mother's womb
Before lying them, lonely, in the cold of a tomb
Toss in the greed of we who have plenty
While we fail to share with people so hungry
Especially the children with stomachs so empty
Over this lay our desire for peace and serenity
With no time to be still in our frenzied activity.

When millions are spent on fancy new schemes
While other men live on the fabric of dreams
Tip over this the plans of nations to make war with each other
Will it be just, or unjust, to bring suffering
To young and old if a different religion or faith they hold?
Will peace never come, must there forever be war?

Whenever our sins are cast into that hole
Be sure we will find there are so many more
The list is endless for we have made it so
A lifetime of sins, will they fill that great space?
Humanity's crimes
Will they all fit into that big black hole?

But we have before us a path to follow:
To look at the suffering of Jesus, to wonder anew at such love
He took our sins on His shoulders
His life paid the price for us all
His blood flowed over that great black hole
Which holds the sins of the human race
Lord, we pray, forgive us our sins
Take our hearts and pour Your love in
May Your healing love wash away our shame
Till the world becomes a most heavenly place
And Jesus be praised
By every nation and race.

                              Amen.

Barbara J Evans

Oh Gentle Mary

Oh gently Mary, what did you see
Upon that tree at Calvary?
Was it the little babe who sat upon your knee
Or the walking man of Galilee
Who raised the dead and multiplied the bread
But had nowhere to lay His head?

When they ran out of wine He gave them a sign
That truly proved your Son was divine.
Oh tell me, Mary, what did He say
Upon that Resurrection Day?
Did He tell you He had come back to stay
And banish all your cares away?

Caroline McKechnie

One Day - Through Life

Dear world, as a babe you are fresh, clean and new
The last star fades in the clear, sparkling dew
A pale dawn shines out and the bird chorus starts
Arise pure, free and refreshed with a grateful heart.

Dear world of youth, in the hard battle of the day
As life races on in a relentless way
Pray for peace, joy and freedom for our fellow man
Regardless of colour, clime, creed or clan.

Dear world, so mature in the late afternoon
A day almost gone, yet still finely in tune
With the dear things of life and the pleasures they bring
Like the warmth of a family or the rebirth of spring.

Dear world, you've grown old, the late shadows fall
You are thankful and happy to have given your all
To dream of great fêtes that have long since gone
And to ponder with pride on a job well done.

Throughout childhood and whether old or mature
Reach out with friendship and love to be safely assured
Rewards will be endless, great bounties unfurl
For faith, hope and compassion can spin our dear world.

Doreen Goodway

Friendship

Friendship, the merging of souls.
More precious than the purest of pearls.
Harder to find, and rarer too.
A beam of untainted light shining through.

Friendship, the flow of dreams
A patch of happiness with flawless seams
A touch of magic, the first rays of sun
A thread of memories come undone.

Friendship, a remedy for strife;
Friends, a blessing, essential for life.

Zarmala Naeem (10)

Hope

I sit and I wonder
I wonder about God
I wonder about life
I wonder about me

I wonder about lost opportunities
And all the hurt I have caused.
I think of time wasted, words never spoken.
I think of a future that I am not in control of.

I sit and wonder if God wonders about me
And if He has regrets about creating me.

Then I look around me and I see Him in everything,
In the sun, in the sea and in the people around me.
He is that stillness amidst the bustle.

Then I take a deep breath and realise that He makes things
New again, He is the God of new beginnings, of second chances.
I look in the mirror and see Him and I know that He will finish
The work that He has started in me. There is yet hope.

Johan Botha

Friend

When your spirit is weak and your faith is running low
When you're looking to the hills and it seems that help comes slow
When you feel prayer stops at your ceiling, you're growing
increasingly numb, losing feeling
When you feel you're nearing your end
Then it's time to call on a friend.

I'll be the one who'll help ease your load
I'll be the one who'll help you down the road
I'll be the one who'll pray in your stead
Until God comes through, I'll carry you.

Rufaro Ruredzo

God

When you are God,
The world crumbles around Your feet,
The sun expands and scorches the Earth,
Your people die because of the heat!

But it's great being God,
Because as well as being on high,
While the world around falls and dies,
You're still standing there alive!

Some people don't believe You're there,
They favour ignorance over truth,
But I know You're there, high and mighty,
No matter who will lose.

So keep your chin up, God,
We need You to protect us,
The sun's still there, the world's not bare,
And God, don't make a fuss.

Those who don't believe,
Still know You're there inside,
They, like me, still love You for it,
Protecting us from high!

Matt Taylor

Atmospheric Layering

Air below the mountain top, blows on secret paths
Flows here obsessively through the sky,
Flows quietly into the sunlight guided by laws,
Incandescent motes, and tiny particles lit
Here below the mountain and above the houses of the village
And the air below the mountain top blows on secret routes.

M Courtney Soper

Journey's End

When someone we love dear passes away
We know we shall remember that day
But in the quiet we recall the past
Full of wonderful memories that will forever last
Memories that will heal the sorrow
And give us strength for all the tomorrows
Familiar faces and places we find
Conjure up happy images left behind
So many images that could fill a book
And when we feel down we can take a look
Life has to go on, we know it must
To deal with things left to us in trust
We rarely get a chance to say goodbye
Before our loved one is beckoned on high
Back to our Maker after a life worthwhile
Only on loan, journey's end, the last mile.

Jan Collingwood

I Yearn

There are many things in life that I wish for
Here and there, I thrive to make ends meet
Earnestly, I yearn for better living
Living life as I give glory to God
More often than not, I praise and worship Him
Against my enemies he fights my battles.

Success, victory, happiness and eternity is found in Him
His word provides strength for me
Under His comfort I find happiness, completeness
My life is incomplete without His presence
Before his eyes I am special
As I yearn for more good things found in Him.

Milton Shoriwa

God Creates - Man Mutilates

I can recall the bluebell woods where I played so long ago.
I returned and asked folk where they were, but no one
seemed to know.
Just rows and rows of houses with strips of concrete everywhere.
Saw no woodland creepy-crawlies, no butterflies dancing in the air.
Man has done away with bluebell woods, he has redesigned the land.
Has destroyed what was so beautiful, tho' he doesn't understand.
Has put his hand on animals, rearranged what was so fair.
I call it 'Mutilation', but Man will say 'tis 'Care'.
Man has criticised God's creation, calls it flaws he will repair.
Once he's done his alterations those who know the truth
will just despair.
Look at the men and women who change the form of their face.
Can't they see their error of judgement? What was noble
they have replaced.
When Man interferes with perfection there is a price he'll have to pay.
He'll become aware when it's too late, he'll hold his head and
rue the day.
Oh God!

Rosie Hues

I See A Person Bending

I see a person bending beneath a heavy load
So many 'whys' and 'wherefores' are in that burden stowed
Each day the weight is growing, the back more crooked, bent
Despairing and despondent, the heart within is rent

But outstretched hands are waiting, within each laden day
A whispering voice is pleading, upon the darkened way
'Give up your burdens, dear one, just hand it o'er to me
Then you will walk uprightly, the way more clearly see!'

Oh change the 'whys' and 'wherefores' to let God's will be done
For, child, when they are lifted, 'tis half the battle won
The load is so much lighter, the path more smooth ahead
When God doth bear beside you, the crushing weight of lead.

Jennifer R Daniel

Everyday Miracles

No money lays within my pocket
No jewels swing across my chest
Sweet hope is my golden locket
In the currency of dreams who shall have less

I have seen a miracle and so could you
It's no shining light nor parting of seas
Simply live with a smile and you shall witness them too

Take a moment to watch the birds
While they glide through a summer's breeze
Their gentle voices can be heard
My friend, you need no wings to be freed

Live for today
Look for tomorrow
The past is all behind

My miracle today is you
For reading this poem of mine

Thank you

Clark Chapman

Untitled

May Heaven bless all those who love
And pardon those who hate
Grant patience to the hasty
And give thanks for those who wait
May all creatures be to us as nearest kin
Greatest mammal to tiny ant
Grant us contentment with our lot
And help to those in want.

Marji Tomlinson

Reflections

Years are passing by
and people try
to fill their time

It is an eternal strife
to make the best of life
during its time

The clock ticks along
day and night belong
to the moods of time

Youth in its prime
like a flower in spring
that fades within time

It is fate's play
to keep age as prey
of time

From start to the end
life is at hand
limited by time . . .

Wila Yagel

Going Home

A wise man said to me,
A wise man made me see,
'Do not suppose you own their life,
A guardian's all you be.

A life that's weak or strong,
A life that's short or long,
The time will come to let it go,
To falter would be wrong.

So, when that time is here
Shed a quiet tear
But say 'au revoir' and not 'goodbye'
They're going home, my dear.'

Elaine Frances

My Prayer For You

May the Lord hear you
When you call
May He hold you
Lest you fall
May you feel His
Love surround you
And His strong arm
Close around you
May He guard you
Night and day
Keep you on the narrow way.
May you lift His banner high
Sing His praise
As days go by
From youth to age
And all life through
May He take good care of you.

P A Fazackarley

Conviction

There is peace in the night,
To relinquish the fight,
To lean back in time,
There is peace in the night,

Restless and yearning,
The heat of the day,
Longing returning,
Restless and yearning.

There is peace in the night,
Let us relish it quite,
To dream with delight,
There is peace in the night.

Mary Hughes

God's Mercy

This world, dear Lord, is full of strife
You breathed on it, you gave if life
Your plan for Man then went astray
When we did sin, did not obey
Man's fall from grace Your heart did sadden
You cast us out of Eden's garden
No more to walk on hallowed ground
To a world where pain and anguish abound
To toil and sweat beneath the sky
To suffer pain and then to die
A Redeemer You sent to save us, Lord
He healed the sick, He preached the word
He died for us upon a tree
On a lonely hill named Calvary
His precious blood did cleanse our sin
A new life then we could begin
Dear Lord, with grace our souls enhance
That we may not discard this second chance.

E V Sherry

Bedtime Prayer

I'm sorry, Lord, for the wrongs I've done,
And for things I should not have said,
I pray for Your forgiveness now,
As I lay me down to bed,

I ask that you watch over me,
My friends and family too,
Grant us peace and rest, oh Lord,
Till the day is born anew.

Matthew R Worthington

Mother

A mother is a precious jewel
You only have the one
You think she's there forever
Then suddenly she's gone.

All the things she's done for you
Down throughout the years
All the laughter and the joy -
Then suddenly the tears.

Lay the flowers on her grave
Tell her of your love
Then suddenly you realise
She's watching from above.

She has not gone completely
She is still in mind and heart
So dry the tears and think of her
You'll never be apart.

Jean Hands

Bedtime

As I prepare to snuggle down
Within my bed (so cosy-warm)
I pray that angels grant me rest
And keep me safe from evil harm.

Thus through the starry moonlit night
I slumber - comforted by thoughts
That Mary and her Saviour Son
Enfold me in their loving arms.

So I awake to greet the dawn
Knowing that I've been with God
Ready now to face a day
Helping others conquer stress.

Steve Glason

Cups

There are these days so many cups
For which in sport, women and men
Strenuously compete.
Football's World Cup at last was won,
Golf's Ryder Cup has come and gone,
Tennis success at Wimbledon
Is a cup-winning feat.

I have some cups I treasure more,
Which none may take away,
Not earned by anything I've done.
My cup of blessings, every day,
Is refilled, used, not locked away,
Polished and only for display.
Blessings are given, not won!

Sometimes the cup that I pick up
Holds suffering, a bitter cup
I taste reluctantly.
But it too is a gift I share,
An ugly cup, found everywhere,
Common in many lives, not rare,
Yet unique, as given to me.

At church, I take a cup divine:
The Covenant Cup, in symbol wine,
Partaking of Christ's blood.
He took the cup of suffering
And made Himself an offering
For all our sins, new life to bring,
Conquering evil with good.

Nancy Solly

Carry On

At times when you feel troubled -
when happiness is gone -
look to the heart within you
for the strength to carry on.

In your heart you will find virtues
such as faith and hope and love.
Three gifts that have been sent you
from a power up above.

It is faith that keeps on searching
for the joy the heart hopes for.
It is love that heals the spirit,
making it stronger than before.

And if your heart be broken -
if your strength should fade away -
the power of these virtues
will still win out the day.

Remember when you're troubled -
when happiness is gone -
look to the heart within you
for the strength to carry on.

Tom Krause

Family

The day the doctor told me,
'In three months, he'll be gone',
My heart broke into splinters
As I sat there alone.

But my two sisters told me,
'Ah, no, you're not alone.
For with us here beside you,
You're never on your own.'

Both they and all their families
Reorganised each day,
So they could help and hold me
As my husband slipped away.

And now they all enfold me
With kindness, love and care.
In everything they do now
They ask me, too, to share.

Their sons and daughters, partners,
Grandchildren laughing with me.
I thank God every day for
My precious family.

Mary Robertson

Light Of Friendship For Ellen

I have seen the light
And it's in you
In everything you are
And in everything you do

It's a perfect light
That shines for all to see
it radiates from you
And has pierced the heart of me

The light is from a friend
It's a light that keeps me warm
It lets me know how loved I am
And keeps me safe from harm

To you, my friend, I am thankful
In each and every way
For you lift my spirits up
With each passing day.

E Lowis & Marina Reeves

The Missionary

('Preach the gospel always; if necessary, use words.' St Francis of Assisi)

An eternal missionary make of me, O Lord:
That Thou be better known because of me,
Be better loved and honoured because of me,
Be seen in flesh and blood again through me.

Benjamin Takavarasha

Summer

Welcome high summer with days of full light,
Trees in their fullness, birds soaring in flight;
But why should we mourn when the golden months fade?
Secure in our 'castles' we have it all made . . .
Heating and lighting, unlimited choice
Of foodstuffs available, no warning voice
To tell us of crippling famine or drought
As befall those who starve and struggle without
Medical, food and water supplies
So far away we can't hear their cries.
In parts of the world where disasters prevail,
Robbed of shelter and nourishment multitudes ail.
All we can do is proffer donation,
So little in face of their dire deprivation,
Thankful for *our* fate, security, care,
Stability during each month of the year,
No earthquakes, volcanoes, no famine or drought
Reminding us all without any doubt
What fortune we have to be born in the west
Where there's always a future in which to invest,
Giving thoughts for the suffering, gratitude too
For this golden summer and regrowth anew.

Rosemary Miller

Never Too Late

(Dedicated to a very dear friend)

It's *never* too late, to hang on to your dreams,
Don't ponder upon what might have been.
Life deals you a card from out of the pack,
You *need* to go *forward,* but, sometimes look back.
Your path has been chosen, the race you *will win,*
Live life to the full, and *never give in!*
Grey clouds may consume you, and darkness befall,
But, sunshine *will* follow, so heed to its call.
At the end of the tunnel, a light will shine through,
It's *never too late* for your dreams to come *true!*

Heather Overfield

God's Mission . . . Just For You!

Don't wish for what you have not got
Or what you cannot do,
But look within your heart and find
God's mission . . . just for you.

With each new day when you awake,
You know that He is there
To hear you say . . . 'I love You, Lord'
And offer up your prayer.

In health or sickness, youth or age,
With seeing eyes or blind,
You are unique - a child of God,
Be that - and you will find . . .

As long as there is life in you,
Each breath you draw forms part
Of what God has designed for you,
Implanted in your heart.

Nanette Mary

Cherished Peace

Aylesford Priory, founded 1242,
The first, Friar Carmelites, given manor
By Richard De-Grey Crusader,
Visionary, St Simon Stock, saw 'Our Lady'
Promising her protection to those
Wearing Carmelite (habit),
Father Malachy, conceived idea (open air shrine).

Sculptors professed, 'A prayer in stone,'
Creating a place of peace, beautiful lawns,
Calm lake, an architectural dream,
Canadian geese rest on the bank,
Weeping willows shelter black-headed gulls,
A very erect black swan swims by.

In the arena, Hadleigh salvation, songsters,
Maidstone band, delight,
Their background 'Florence' in appearance,
The breathtaking blue mosaic shrine, arched alcoves.

Compelled by love, the singers harmoniously sing,
Guest Kerry Sampson sings, 'All I ask of you',
Nicholas Lester sings tunes from Oklahoma
In an operatic style.

Ann dynamically twirling big drum skilfully,
Lone trumpeter plays on the roof 'Last Post',
Sun now setting, I looking back, now dark,
Lit up the beautiful shrine,
A day to cherish.

Patricia Turpin

Perfection

I come with a deep sense of Your perfection,
Your purity, Lord.
I worship Your unblemished perfection.
You need no embellishment,
nothing mere humanity can add.
Perfect just as You are,
and always have been;
never changing, pure through and through.
Light unimaginable,
more than Man's highest wisdom can grasp.
Holy awe, speechless, breathless awe,
fills my consciousness, Lord,
as I catch just a glimpse of Your purity.
How this perfection draws me.
How it stills my spirit.
The essence of Your purity fills a deep need in Man,
who is drawn to beautiful perfection.
Lord, Your love is perfect,
You love this weak and wayward sinner perfectly,
as only You can.
Perfection and imperfection meet,
as a soul indwelt
in love with its Creator; is satisfied.

Jeannette Facchini

My Summer Visitor

Hopping onto a patio pot,
My friendly robin waits,
Till I move to tend the trough
Where he comes to gaze at me,
As if to say 'What's for me today?'

I left him pondering there,
While I went off poste haste,
To ask the local pet shop man,
'What do robins like for a treat?'

Down off the shelf came a plastic box
With . . . mealworms!
Covered in meal, they squiggled and squirmed,
So, it was, with great aplomb, I paid,
And took my dangerous cargo home.
What if they got out? They'd multiply!
A garden full of mealworms - oh no!

Tightly lidded, in the shed they went,
Come morning, carefully opening the box,
I spooned a few onto a dish and watched,
Ere long my friend got wind of it;
In he flew, and perched and ate his fill.

Thus it was for two days more,
It gave me such a kick;
And then he didn't appear.
I heard he'd found much better fare
In a garden, with pond, three doors up.

It was a bit of a blow,
But in my shed are not so -
Squiggly, squirming mealworms,
They're going for a song,
A robin's song of course!

Jean McPherson

Faith

Faith to trust
Faith to simply believe
Faith to be true
Faith to show a love that's real
Faith to walk with me
Faith to face the future
Faith is to be loyal
Faith is trustworthy
Faith is a fulfilling trust
Faith is a cure
Faith is a healing
Faith is to cope
Faith is the power of faith
Faith is a strong foundation
Faith is loving grace and care
Faith and still have faith
Faith and keeping it did the trick
Faith gives birth to joy in you
Faith you touched me
Faith in your love and power
Faith bringing happiness to all
Faith be comforted have no fears
Faith with healing of hands
Faith with Him who cares
Faith changes lives for everyone
Faith eyes fixed on, God above
Faith the world will appear brighter
Faith believe all will be well
Faith and hope love will never give up
Faith for God's blessing that He brings.

Rita Scott

The Old Lie

God rot the souls
Of those who swear
That truth is beauty.

For what is there
To beguile the sight
In dull-eyed palisades
Of empty smiles?

What can be found
That's fair, in a place
Of ghosts, alone,
Loitering on concrete corners,
The dust of long-dead dreams
Swirling round their feet?

No, beauty lies,
Knee-deep in that
Sweet perversity,
That fools call friendship;
Beauty lies.

Rad Thomas

Live Each Day

Don't waste time
Seek out pleasures in your life
Live and enjoy each day to the fullest
And feel great then you will feel great
And live a great life.

Joan Clothier

Cosy

Listen to the pitter-patter
Of the rain
As it drips and drops
Upon the rooftop,
Splashes into scattered puddles
And trickles down a liquid street.

Hear the gentle
Swishing sound
Of an easy wind
That blows upon a chilly winter's night.

And I huddle myself
Into a little ball,
Curled up tightly in my bed,
Deep under my warm, thick blankets.
Like a foetus in a womb.

So comfortable and content,
So still and at peace,
So snug and cosy.

Declan Mullan

Discovery

I heard the music
But never knew that I could dance
Until I moved my feet
If I could feel my freedom
Oh! I'm sure I could fly.

Bill Campbell

Life

When life seems to get you down
Don't give up and wear a frown,
Remember just along the way
There'll be a much more brighter day.

For every tear that you shed
A smile is waiting up ahead,
Just have hope and you will see
Dreams will become a reality.

There is always help on hand
From those who've gone to the spirit land,
They will guide you from above
And wrap you in their warmth and love.

This dark pathway that you tread
Will turn into light up ahead,
Live each new day with love and hope
Knowing your loved ones will help you cope.

So when the going gets too rough
And you feel you've had enough,
Close your eyes and they'll be here
With loving thoughts to give you cheer.

Margaret Anne Hedley

Your Church?

The spires point up to the heavens,
Strength through solid walls that will last;
Gothic beauty displayed for all seasons,
Treasures indeed from the past.

Over centuries a true holy haven,
Countless millions have gathered in prayer;
Vicars offered their sacred comfort
To the hundreds who worshipped God there.

But today? Well just look around you;
Is the Christian voice muted and blurred?
Too many pews are left empty;
So why isn't the word being heard?

Do too many Christians keep silent,
Not speaking their faith to a friend?
Are they fearful of seeming different,
Of bucking the secular trend?

The church is not just pretty windows,
Nor a building set fair into view;
The Church needs to spread joy around it,
For, Christian, the real Church is *you!*

John Stephens

Always Assured

(Psalm 23. Isaiah 9:6)

The Lord is my shepherd, I have everything I need,
Even when I walk the valley of death
He's there to accompany His sheep.
I will not be afraid, His umbrella of love covers me.
All the way He leads and reassures 'for free'.

His promises last forever, His words mean what they say.
E'en though the path with trouble fraught
He'll stay with you always.
Shepherds call their flock who recognise familiar tones
Following closely in trust, winding the track safely home.

Praise the Lord, He's wonderful,
Eternal life is given
To all the 'flock' who wear the badge
Of salvation in Jesus' name.

Annie R Harcus

Today Is Now

Saving your tomorrow is just a waste of time,
Today is now, so use it while you can.
Tomorrow is a promise, without reason, without rhyme.
Today is new, untouched, without a plan.

A new day, a new adventure unfolds with each sunrise,
Make the most of every single hour,
And when the day is over, you'll find to your surprise
Your smiles have chased away that April shower.

Show a happy smiling face to each and every one
Though in your heart you have to hide your fears,
And very soon behind the clouds you'll see the morning sun,
So greet each day with happiness, not tears.

Don't waste a single moment of that bright new sunny day,
Life is for the living don't you know.
The world will laugh right with you if you just show the way,
And you'll find your troubles soon will go.

Mary Davies

Do Not Bury Your Hopes

When you feel pain, do not bury your hopes.
The end of your long road is not yet here.
When it thunders and rains, you can cope.
That's what the song says, you take care.
I found an obstruction some years ago
And life seemed to me to be unfair.
But I found a solution; confidence can grow,
As if in a dream, from somewhere.
I buried my face, but then I smiled.
I searched for God and wept in joy.
First I lost my race, after many miles.
I faced the flood but then success buoyed.
When faced with the odds, don't feel crushed.
You can somehow make things work.
I know it feels odd, still just brush
Away your frown and light a spark.

Muhammad Khurram Salim

Gone

If he was here now he'd be seven
If he was here now he'd be son
If he was here now he'd be top of his tree
If he was here now . . . but he's gone
If he was here now, would he look like me?
If he was here now would he care?
If he was here now would it be different?
We'd have more than memories to share
If he was here now he'd say 'Thank you,'
If he was here now he'd say 'Mum
I'll always be looking down on you
As my life has only begun.'
So as I sit here with my reflections
Daily he goes through my head
The son I never had from birth
Is my son I'll never forget

Dean Squires

Untitled

According to Godde's universal planne
Whilst on this Earthe shall each and every manne
Have unto him awarded a lyffe spanne
A given time of three score years and ten.

But each manne in this grate and wond'rous worlde
Wille hath for him his owne such length unfurled;
Sum hav been barely cast, sum longwayes hurled,
And sum exactly three score years and ten.

But ours be notte the choyce, ours notte to knowe
When for us cums the Reaper; when to go.
And cum he wille as sure as tyde must flowe
Before or after three score years and ten.

So if thou hast survived this spanne of lyffe
Thank ye they Godde for that gudmanne, gudwyffe
And take thy ease, with sound of drum and fyffe
To live beyond they three score years and ten.

Andrew Ferrie

Thank You, Lord

Thank you, Lord, for giving me this day,
to do as I want and to live come what may,
for giving me time to remember years past
and pray that the future will not go so fast.

Thank you, Lord, for listening to me
for whenever I pray, my words are a plea,
please help when I call, when feelings are low,
be there as my anchor and never let go.

Thank you, Lord, for friends caring and true
who come to our aid with help sent from You,
be with us each day in thought, word and deed
and stay close beside us whatever our need.

Jim Pritchard

Let's Not Waste Any More Time . . .

There are times in our lives
When we take stock of everything
Everything that we take for granted
The people around us and everything we have
But it's not until suddenly something or someone is no longer there
We realise just how much they did for us and meant to us
Did they know just how much a part of our lives they were?
Did we ever tell them? Probably not.
So let's not waste any more time
Take a moment out of our busy day
To tell those we love how much they mean to us
Because it just might be the last time you see them
Who knows what lies ahead in our lives?
They could be taken all too suddenly
And that precious time is lost
They are gone, forever
And we will never have the chance again to say 'I love you'
So when life is hectic and we get stressed out
Take a moment with a loved one, for a hug or a kind word
It will suddenly put everything into perspective
They are the ones who are most important in your life.

Jacqui Watson

Thinking Of You

Somewhere in the world
Someone is thinking of you
It could be someone you know
Or someone you knew
Maybe remembering a moment you shared
That goes to show how much they cared
Sometimes it's sad when we let people go
But we never stop thinking of people we know
If only we knew they were thinking of us
Maybe we'd visit and jump on a bus
There are so many people you meet in a day
Some of them stay and some drift away . . .

Anne-Marie Howard

Reflection In The Mirror

The reflection in the mirror has a story to be told
The mind is ever young but the face is growing old,
First there are memories of happy days with mother
Happy, busy days without a little brother!
Cooking and sewing and then we'd stop for tea,
Father far away at war, sailing on the sea.

Then there were the teen years filled with happiness and strife
Earning a living before becoming wife.
Next the wedding day, another phase in life to face
More skills and learning, acquiescence with good grace.
Suddenly a big change, the biggest one by far
A baby on the way, now we'll need a car.

Then the mewling bundle lying in the arms
Fast grown to a toddler, motherly alarms.
All too soon the young are growing up too
Those childhood years, they are so very few.
Now they're off to college, mother's life, she has it back
A desert island is appealing, a grass and leaf shack!

Now we're planning weddings, the children's that is
Mother is redundant, life has lost its fizz - or has it?
With time on her hands, her own interests she can follow
Whether in the garden or in a bubble bath to wallow.
Maybe she'll travel or take a course or two
Other women do it - it's quite the thing to do.

Mother is once more a woman, to be wined and dined
The company academic - a little more refined,
She has found her own way, so what if there are lines?
She's enjoying her third age - keeping up with the times.
The reflection still is there looking back at me
I wonder what experiences, next time I look, I'll see.

Yvonne Bulman-Peters

Woven Threads

Bereavement,
Affects us all at some point in our lives,
And the word death, for some, signals the end,
Yet the spirit minus its physical outer garment,
Continues its sojourn,

The essence and energy,
Wrought at the Creator's hand,
Builds a living tapestry,
Which spans the divide,
Between this world and the next,

We, the threads that are woven,
Into the picture that constantly changes,
Thoughts and memories,
Are the strands that still connect us
To those who have made the journey,

Love is the hand
That stitch by stitch,
Side by side
For millennia,
Has embroidered a new image,

Beyond the barriers,
Of earthly time,
Another chapter of existence unfolds,
Where one day we too will join those,
Who went just a short way ahead,

In the realms where only light exists,
We will meet our loved ones in perfect peace and harmony,
A new voyage awaits us all,
Life is everlasting,
For what designer would destroy its creations?

Ann G Wallace

A Brighter Tomorrow

There is a goodness that shines deep within
Every soul who repents their life of sin;
An energy pure, with its roots deep in love;
A guidance from angels in Heaven above.

Have faith in your feelings, they help you to learn,
Take each of them in and accept them in turn.
Is it happiness, joy and love that you feel
Or sorrow, or anger, sometimes all too real?

Then act on these feelings, change those which cause pain;
You have much to lose, yet everything to gain.
Be brave and confront your innermost fears,
Don't hide and feel worthless for wasting your years.

There's no time like the present for turning a new leaf,
The unique person you are needs to have this belief;
A belief so alluring that it pulls you along
Then calms every fear to make you feel strong.

Satan or evil will sometimes hold sway
So let God, through Jesus, show you the way.
For this is the path you can choose to follow;
The only one leading to a brighter tomorrow.

Tracey Lynn Birchall

Oasis

Lay a little time aside each day
To still your aching mind and watch the world run on for a while.
And if your world still calls
Hang a picture of your kind of heaven on the fridge door,
Tape contented memories by your space at work,
Keep your peace close
So it becomes a real part of your day.

Lay a little time aside for God each morning
And, like a well-loved friend,
In time, you'll learn the sound of His voice as He knows yours.
Be still, be silent, be absorbed and comforted,
And if your world still calls
Hang on to His fragrance
So He remains a real part of your day.

Lay a little time aside for an oasis whenever you can.
For in a world where speed is of the essence
We could be in danger
Of running past the very reason we exist.
And if we miss the reason
We're running in the wrong direction.

Tracey Kesterton

Living A Lie

Living a lie, I had to do
So it would please every one of you,
Living a lie, I did not like,
Cos it caused me such a fight,
Peace of mind I had to give,
This did not come from within.

Ready for this I was not,
Wished I had not done this lot,
Forced and pushed, yes I was,
Even I could not handle this,
Living a lie for every one of you,
Now I am paying through and through.

'Can the Lord forgive me?' I say.
'Will the pain ever go away?'
Make someone happy, they say to me,
So she could die peacefully,
Now I did this for every one of you.

Now look what they've gone and done,
They have split one and all,
Who really cared at all?
Only one, this I know,
God bless her wherever she goes,
That's my sister, Jo.

She gave to me more than anyone,
Because she knew what I had done,
She gave to me the reason to lie,
She also knew I couldn't cry,
Cos she knew the pain I carried inside
For living that lie.

Irene Stevens

Our Vows

Just eleven months after we met
We went to the church to wed
Eleven months didn't seem long and yet
Together we stood before God and said
We'd love each other completely
No other would come between
That we would be faithful to each other
In the good times and the lean
In all our years together
Neither of us went astray
And we have loved each other
Right from the very first day
We grew closer and closer together
Never wanting to be apart
We knew each other inside out
From deep within our hearts
We both had kept our promise
Never having a thought to stray
It's true God didn't make us a promise
But I never thought he would say
You've had a good life together
Then come and take you away
But remember this, my darling
My promise to you remains true
I shall only stay here a short while
Then I'll travel home to you

Daphne Fryer

Our Kitchen Table

Many conversations
Many secrets bared
Lots of tears and laughter
Many troubles shared

Lots of worries have been eased
As much as we've been able
Lots of problems have been solved
Around our kitchen table

Countless snacks and cups of tea
Soup served with a ladle
Dreams and hopes and sympathy
Around our kitchen table

We hope our children now they're grown
Will have a table of their own
So that their children will be able
To chat around the kitchen table

Sylvia Dyer

A Little Prayer

Each night when I go to bed
I say a little prayer
For the whole wide world
And the people living there

I pray that one day
All the stupid wars will end
And everyone will walk
Hand in hand as friends

So please, dear Lord above
Shower this world of mine
With happiness and love
And then all the wars may end
Then everyone may walk
Side by side
As each other's friend.

Donald Tye

Love's Regret

When first your charm and beauty I beheld.
My praise and love were oft withheld.
By stubborn pride and arrogant mind.
The lack of love was so unkind.

My eyes that now are so unclear,
Did see much brighter, things not near.
So many deeds to have been done,
But only selfish things begun.

My ears that now reject all sound,
Should oft have heard your voice profound.
And strayed not into other ways,
Of sleepless nights and sinful days.

Teach us oh! Thou power divine,
In our youth these gifts are Thine.
That thoughts and eyes and ears and ways,
May ever more reflect Thy praise.

K Blomley

The Road

A road that promised much
Stretched itself in front of me
But led to hidden corners
And had ruts I couldn't see,
Trees bowed across and turned it
To a tunnel with no end
Into its darkened hopelessness
I could feel myself descend.
Alone beside this road I sat
All thoughts of progress gone
Until I heard one single voice
That made me carry on;
Truth is, wherever a road may lead
That single voice is all you need.

Jen Housden

Life

When life is a burden and getting you down
Don't be down-hearted and please don't frown
Trials and tribulations may beset you on life's way
But despite that, you are lucky, as you go along each day

No hurricane, tsunami or starvation waiting here
We live, we breathe, we laugh (or cry) with nothing much to fear
Our needs are met and even though we think we may want more
Let's face it, if we look closely, we really know the score

No child has died, through no fault of our own
No house is lost, no crop that lovingly we have sown
No husband, wife or lover has expired before our eyes
Or even worse, is lost without us knowing where she lies

Count blessings daily, thank the good Lord up above
That we have managed thus far to survive, armed with His love
And at the end of life, long or short as it may be
Say 'Thank you, Lord' for caring and for giving life to me.

Liz Maskill

Summer

The summer has come, spring's gone away,
There's laughter of children, when they're at play.
We hear the sound of the birds, the buzzing of bees,
The breeze gently caressing the leaves on the trees.
There's no need for words as we walk hand in hand,
Silence is golden as we stroll through God's land.
We climb over the hills as we go on our way,
Smell the rich earth and the newly mown hay.
Walk down to the sea where the gulls swoop down low
And hear the crash of the waves at the tide's ebb and flow.
Nature painted a picture for us to see
Of a wonderful landscape for you and for me.
So let the memories linger on, let them remain,
So together we can walk through that picture again . . .

Derek Burt

The Outcast

The fox is seen as a cunning one
Despised as a base creature under this sun
No sympathy or compassion comes his way
In fact, cruelty is often part of his day
And when stealth becomes a habit, to survive
It affects your behaviour, as you constantly strive
To nurture and protect your young from the foe
When all they really want is to hurt you so
No court of session here, to apportion blame
Only poison and traps, to kill or maim
And when the odds are stacked as high as this
Then maybe a little kindness would not be remiss
For it is foretold, the lion will lie down with the lamb
So maybe the hen and fox can share the same pram
And who knows, maybe mankind will also aspire
To share their supper, with all who desire
The way forward in accepting the Lord's command
To love another, all across the land.

Anon

A Friend Like You

In moments of complete despair
When life seems to be so unfair
And all I want to do is die
I take one look at you and sigh
For if I have a friend like you
How could I feel the way I do?
I'm wrong to feel life's not worth living
Or that love's not worth the giving
It's worth every day of pain
To see your smile just once again

Georgina Paraskeva

Lying In A Hospital Bed

I'm lying in a hospital bed
covered in bruises from toe to head.
I'm leaking in a dozen places
my legs are like balloons
my back is breaking and
my muscles are screaming
will we ever be right again?

Another injection, another drip
blood swabs and tissue tests
scans and X-rays, blood and tears.

Dislocation, dislocation is a
word I hear bandied about.
You mustn't do this and you mustn't do that
don't bend forward and don't bend sideways
just keep lying flat on your back.
My body and I are asking in fear
will we ever be right again?

Then a host of angels hovering close by
whispered softly in my ear
'Your surgeon and your anaesthetist
have been sent by the power of light.
They are special. The very best
to perform a miracle of healing.
Though your body is delicate
your spirit and will are strong
the day will come when the pain is gone
and you will rejoice again in love and life.'

My heart filled with wonder and delight
for indeed the surgeon and anaesthetist
are angels in disguise.
Words of thanks are not enough
to express the feelings inside
nevertheless, please accept my heartfelt
gratitude for the wonderful
care you lavished on me

Brigitta D'Arcy-Hays

Circumstance

You came - by pure chance
And sent my fluttering heart a-dance,
Although you could not stay for very long,
You set my frame beating with merry song,
With promises not meant to keep
And sweetest dreams invading my sleep,
Oh where are you now?

Do your thoughts ever return,
With longing, your aching heart to yearn
For that one heady day when we first met
And I found myself forever in your debt?
As you turned on a bridge, going away,
Out of my life for many a day,
Do you ever think of me?

Do you recall, at eventide,
That small village church, side by side,
Sitting closely together, within love's deep spell,
And I sang 'Avé Maria' to echoing sweet bells,
Our hands touched, lingered warm awhile,
As we turned to each other, shyly, to smile,
Oh surely you remember?

When I picture the highest hills,
Stepping stones and fast-gurgling rills,
Mountains, valleys, forests, green byways,
I am striding along with you, filling my days
With longing thoughts of 'might have been',
Had we two met sooner on life's scene,
Our hearts entwined forever.

Julia Eva Yeardye

God's Waiting Room

The residential home was hushed and still
The television sound turned very low
Around the room, high-seated, wing-backed chairs
And over all lamps cast a rosy glow.

Upon the quietness, soft breathing came:
What dreams went through each grey and balding head?
Perhaps of life before, when they were young
Or of a future freed from pain and dread.

An angel hovered quietly above,
Softly he led one soul to heavenly shore.
There to greet his comrades, family, God
And rest in peace with them for evermore.

No sound as medics on thick carpet trod;
And soon was left one single empty chair.
Siesta time was over and they saw
Knowing that someone else would soon be there.

Outside the merry voices rang with glee.
Enjoy your life, for years pass by too soon,
And each and every one of you will be
Waiting quietly in God's waiting room.

Barbara Dunning

Turn Grey Days Into Blue

When you sit in your ivory tower
Thinking your life has lost all of its power
And sitting thinking you can't go on
Don't just believe the good things are gone

Just one more day will change your mind
At the end of it, you may well find
Life is worth living, it seems after all
The problems you have are really quite small

Think of all the things you have got
Good health is wealth, it means such a lot
So just go outside, see things that there are
I'm sure if you look, you'd be better by far

Just look at the trees, the flowers and the roses
And you'll begin to feel simply quite cosy
That you're getting your life back together again
And you're not feeling in quite so much pain

Go and help someone who's blind
It will help you and heal your mind
You'll think they can't see those things
'I can!' It's a joy, what every day brings
So don't start to shed anymore tears
And then you'll go on living a good many more years.

Sheila Moore

Friendships

When I lay awake each night tossing in my bed
When my mind just won't switch off and all thoughts of sleep have fled
My mind drifts back to days gone by:
To dear friends whom I have known
As long as I have my memories I shall never feel alone.
First friendships formed at Love Lane School
Still treasured and held most dear
How often I still think of them and wish I had them near.
As I moved on reluctantly and left them all behind
I still retained those friendships; they're of the lasting kind!
I've made so many more dear friends at each phase of my life
Through childhood, teens, adulthood, even now in later life.
Good friends have always been there through the good times
And the bad
Their support and friendship most valued at the times
When I've been sad.
Each and all their memories have such a special place
That I pray, as I get older, advancing years will not erase.

Kathleen Stringer Fairburn

Prayer For Today

Father God
Through the dawning
Of this new day
Guide my footsteps
Light my way
Give me the strength
To be
Loving and giving
Thoughtful and kind
To all mankind.
Amen

Penny Kirby

Palm Sunday

(Matthew 21 vs 1 to 10 & Zechariah 9 vs 9)

Spread your cloak, grab a palm,
let's all rejoice and sing a psalm,
praise the Lord, call out with glee,
your Saviour comes astride donkey.
Cry blessings to your Saviour King,
shout aloud, hosannas ring.
Zechariah's word today comes true,
'See your King now comes to you.'
He truly is, God's righteous Son,
salvation's come for everyone.
So spread your cloak, grab a palm,
let's all rejoice and sing a psalm.

Albert E Watson

One Saviour

An offering to God of all the sacrificed,
Of so many faults we all have in our lives,
If there is unfulfilment, then you are lost.
Turn envy into hope for the love of thy Lord Jesus Christ
We all seem to share,
Make all your cares worthwhile.
See how much you can do in your lives.
We all change in our lives,
How much righteousness do we need
Until we all find happiness?
Without freedom we would be proud,
If you can't forgive, you will have a restless soul.
Bless those who are down without help,
When we are given a rough deal,
Try, try and try again.
Jesus Christ never fails.
If we take guilt to God then we release our fears.
There is only one Saviour.

Antoinette Christine Cox

Faith

With love's sweet candle
I light my way
Weaving through time's passage
A sound I hear. I say,

'Who's there?
Do I know thee?'
Heart pounding
Should I flee?

I turn towards the darkness
Holding aloft my light
A snarl, a cry of pain, a whirling wind
And something runs in fright

My journey onwards I continue
The candle safe, shining brighter
The darkness falling behind me
With all its possible horrors

Up ahead my goal becomes clear
A doorway set in a glowing frame
I reach out
Grasp the handle
And pull . . .

Yvonne Carsley

I Wish

I wish I was infectious laughter
spreading to iron out the Earth's miseries
I wish I was a gentle summer breeze
blowing serenity over the world
I wish I was a peaceful ray
radiating peace to all four corners of the Earth.

Dora Watkins

Together Always

We'll be together
Always thro' our lives

Never lonely
With each other by our sides

We'll help each other
In troubled times

Never leave you, my friend
You'll always be mine

We'll be together
Always in our hearts

Help each other out
Never stray apart;

I'll always be here for you
Our friendship : never-ending

Together always
As best friends.

Sarah Grigor

A Prayer For Peace

Bring peace to our land
Oh God
Let Man lay down the sword
May his people
Shake one another's hand
May deluded politicians
No longer rule
May God
Bring peace to this
Troubled world
May the almighty
Hand of God
Make a stand.

Penny Kirby

A Balm To The Soul

My Polish friend has a romantic heart
and a rueful eye, as do I.

We think alike on many things -
how living life now
sometimes brings
a tear to us
or how its better parts
such as our lasting friendship
contribute - as she puts it -
honey in the heart.

At this point in our respective lives
poised as we are
on the threshold of reflection
we exchange our thoughts
on how life has changed
since we ourselves were young
and how such change seems
not always for the best
how the pace of life has quickened
in the futile race for time
and how, with mature eye
we both feel grateful somehow
to be left behind.

We take pleasure in the small things -
shared feelings
minds meeting
seasons fleeting
and the gentle
heating effect of
honey in the heart.

Maureen Horne

Precision Placing

Our lives are like a jigsaw
That we build from day-to-day
There are lots and lots of pieces
To be fitted on the way

Sometimes we find it boring
Just to slot in bits of sky
Or maybe grey of the mountains
That are towering up so high

Some pieces are so colourful
So very gay and bright
And these we love to work on
Just to get the picture right

Could we fit in a kindly deed?
Or find a piece of prayer
A word of comfort to a friend
Who is maybe in despair

It is important that the pieces
All find their proper place
So we must show lots of patience
Keep working with good grace

When our time of Earth is over
And our lives here are no more
Will we leave a pretty picture
Ere we reach that distant shore

Doreen E Todd

God Bless, Goodnight!

I'm new to this, so please don't laugh
I've brushed my teeth and had a bath
And now am trying to go to sleep
But before I start counting sheep
I've got a few things I want to say
So here I go, I'll try to pray . . .
Dear Lord, up there where angels are found
(Oh my God, how cheesy that sounds!)
I want to say thanks for all I've got
(Except the bad hair and massive spot)
I want to say cheers for the great day I've had
(Even though the maths test was pretty bad)
I've opened my eyes to how lucky I am
(I've got a new phone, TV and webcam)
I've got family and really great friends
(I've also got chipped nails, braces and split ends)
But I've realised life is great! It's really a blast!
And I want to say thanks, I hope it will last.
Oh no, that's not a prayer, that's not right
What I'm trying to say is . . .
Thanks, God bless, goodnight!

Kim Akwei-Howe (14)

Choices

Live your life with *love*
Find *joy* in all you do
Make *peace* your goal in life
Patience will see you through
Let your *kindness* shine like a light
May *goodness* show you the way
To your *faithfulness* hold true
Show *gentleness* every day
These are your choices in life
Make them firm, steadfast and true
Then God will reach out and guide you
No matter what you do.

Christine Collins

Could

Save a shilling for a sunny day
So that we can go out and play,
For when the weather is hot,
And the sun high in the sky;
We no longer have to hide inside.

We could go to the coast;
Travel by a ragged old train.
We will stand in the soothing sea breeze,
With some gentle waves upon our bare feet,
Then we could watch the sunrays go to sleep.

We could go to the country;
With a picnic hamper and adventure,
Then lay in the shade under splendid trees,
Wondering of the whys and ifs,
Then we could watch nature settle in dusk's mist.

We could do so many, if only
To save a shilling for a sunny day,
So that we can go away,
Away from the fresh warm smell of decay.

Zeva7

Be Still

If we give little time
to listening
we cannot come into truth

Silence can lead to
stillness in the heart
this can stop the mind racing

Just open your heart
close your eyes
where there is stillness healing is formed

Jean K Washbourne

Test Of Faith

Many things can test our faith,
Ill-health, warfare, a broken home.
All could ask, why me?
And yet at all times we often feel
A presence at our side.

The wonders of life restore our faith,
Yet we always knew that life must have
Its triumphs and disappointments.

The birth of a child brings us happiness,
God has given new life.

All through our lives we must face ups and downs,
Often they come to try us.

God will give us immortal love -
To be with us every day.

At eventide we fall asleep;
With problems left for another day.

When life is over, we meet our Risen Lord
We kneel down there before Him
We have gone from strength to strength
He has led us safely through all.

Janet Cavill

Peace

From out of the mist
A bright light shines
A figure slowly beckons me forward
To step into the light
Transporting me
To a place
Where there's no pain.

Alice Higham

Thought For The Day

When all of this is past
What have I changed about life?
Have I made the world
A better place for being here?
When I am gone
Will somebody still remember me
As the person who made
Their lives
A little easier
Or will they refuse to acknowledge what I am?

In this day
Will I have contributed
To the sum total of human existence and happiness?
Will I have given new insights
To the problems of many
Or will I have helped
Those I love?

In this day will I have become a better person?
Will I have created more
That people can still see?
Will I have set myself a monument
In the thoughts of those that surrounded me?

Alasdair Sclater

Mutual Understanding

I know at the moment the pain seems unreal,
Go towards the pain and work with it, it'll help you heal,
Why these things happen, it's hard to understand,
You *were,* you *are,* so therefore *you can.*

What you do with your life is down to you,
Nobody and nothing can hurt you, unless *you* allow it to,
In the *here and now* the pain is untrue,
How your *spirit* grows, is now down to you.

I can totally relate to you, it's a bitter-sweet pain,
You have to go in to come out, then nothing will never hurt you again,
Time is the healer, so they say,
I'm proof of that saying, I get stronger every day.

You know where I am and believe in you,
It's time for *your spirit to grow,* discover the true you,
The pain never stops but it's put in its place,
One day the pain will be sweet reflections in your secret place.

It's time to believe in yourself, you're a woman who cares,
One day, good moments made into memories, once again
you'll share,
At the end of the day this is another lesson to go into,
It's one of the hardest lessons to learn and it'll all be down to you.

Patricia Deakin

Triumph House - Spiritual Reflections 2007

In This Life

A vision was created through my inner eye;
A wide leafy green river with lush banks
Two cane-woven canoes awaiting two souls
Who could never long be parted.
As I glided downstream the flow was placid and tranquil
Created from my own tears
Shed in grief and despair
In this life.

And then before me the most magnificent lagoon
Crammed with gift-laden ships and boats.
My eyes welled with tears at its significance
I knew I was seeing my afterlife treasures.
For these were my ships
Those that had sailed without me
In this life.

I recognised each one as I floated past
The pain, torment and sadness caused by their sailing
Now replaced by an exalting and deserved joy
In that sanctuary of abundance
Accumulated - for the next -
In this life.

Rita Carter-Forde

Lord, Make Me

Lord, make me beautiful
But not in body or face
Make me ugly, Lord, I pray
Make my beauty into grace

Lord, make me wealthy
Make me rich beyond all measure
Make me affluent in mercy
Let forgiveness be my treasure

Please, Lord, make me clever
Give me intelligence set apart
But not in science, not in business
Let my wisdom be my heart

Lord, make me worthless,
Make me helpless, make me weak
Take everything, Lord, I beg you
And let love be all of me.

Lesley Tuck

Our World

There once was a world like a diamond
So beautiful for all to see
But Man chipped away at this diamond
Only a fragment was left to be
That diamond was so precious
It was so very rare
Man began to realise this diamond needed care
This diamond is our world
And we should treat it so
With love, understanding and kindness
And in time this world will grow

Renalta Hall

Angel On My Shoulder

There's an angel on my shoulder
Which brings me great delight
She's always there to guide me
So I will know what's right.

She is my close companion
I won't let her slip away
I cling to her obsessively
Every single day.

She leads me up to Heaven
And cheers me up no end
Optimism stays with me
She is my special friend.

I trust her implicitly
I lean on her when sad
And feel her arms around me
When things are very bad.

Do you want to know my angel's name
So you won't have to mope?
It's really not a secret
My angel's name is Hope.

Linda Hurdwell

Solo?

Climbers and Arctic explorers often find
they have to finish alone as they near their goal.
Pressing on solo, some feel another presence
journeying with them.
An Emmaus experience, perhaps?

Dorothea Abbott

My Jeans, My Friend

To me,
There is nothing more than a pair of jeans,
To show you who you are.

Like a friend,
Jeans grow with you,
They change with you.

The longer you have them,
The more comfortable they become,
Just like a friend.

The longer you have them,
The more they are appreciated,
Just like a friend.

Jeans are the one thing you know you can rely on,
Something that will make you feel good,
Just like a friend.

Like a friend,
They are always there,
When you need them the most . . .

To you,
There is nothing more than a pair of jeans,
To show you who I am,
Your friend.

Shelley

Leaving

And when I'm gone and buried then
Lay me beneath the heathered glen.

My soul not there 'neath soil so firm
It lifts on gentle breeze to Heaven.

Go now from here and weep no more
Your heart fine memories there be stored.

And think of me in bright sunshine
No cold grey granite for a shrine.

Pass your love to bairns just born
For I will see the summer morn.

Find peace within yourself, my child
Go now and walk in meadows wild.

For that's the place you will find me
Red poppies open for sun to feel
Grasses wave your mind to steal
Were Coney's run and flee.

Nicky Anderson

The Clouds Will Part

Cares like clouds can compass our clear sky,
Hiding from view the radiance of the sun
But let us not forget that by and by
The clouds will part, the sun break through again.

Let us take heart when threatening clouds appear
At times upon the skyline of our lives
And let us never once bow down to fear,
The clouds will part, the sun break through again.

If we should meet someone who's filled with care,
Perhaps a cheery word would help along the way,
Let us this simple truth in kindness share,
The clouds will part, the sun break through again.

Stanley Birch

A New Journey

You took me by the hand from the moment I
Arrived here and revealed the secrets of the
Universe to me. Lovingly wrapping me up
Inside your soul where you kept me safe and warm.

Flying high through the many delightful realms
Of awe and wonder, filling my soul with so much
Love and joy as the magic and beauty enticed my
Whole being to succumb to the gifts that have
Been bestowed upon it.

Overawed by this mighty love that flows
Freely and unconditionally, piercing the
Very heart of my true divine self as the
Truth unfolds itself perfectly all around me.

Feel the essence of your true self embody the whole of your
Being, an integration of wholeness, the transformation begins
Slowly and gently, it is an enchanting and mystical journey of
The soul. Lost in the serenity that surrounds your soul, flowing
On waves of tranquillity, your soul soaks up the life force of nature.

Starchild

A Little Guidance

A gentle soul that is lost can be guided to the right place.
At the appropriate time it can be moulded and it blossoms.
Coming into its own, a voice can be heard,
And a fountain of knowledge is shared with the world.

Ise Obomhense

Do Not Cry

Do not cry, do not fear,
no need to shed a tear.
For where you have gone,
there's peace, there's love,
high above the clouds above.

The world that I have left you in below,
please show that you are strong -
choose your path, live your life,
forgive others who have wronged.

Regrets have gone, mistakes were made,
time now to move on.
Give love to those who need it now,
be strong, oh yes, be strong.

Look in your heart, and inside you'll see
the right way forward now will be.
The future is here and now, don't blame yourself I've gone,
just live your life, go on, go on, just live your life, be strong!

Thésie Jenkinson

Universal Interaction

The dawn is nearing towards cosmic intervention,
Good forces beyond and behind us
Are uniting to balance the world's dissension.
With seeds of peace, harmony and love they will disseminate,
We with faith, strong belief in miracles
Will help to harvest and accumulate.
Together in friendship and trust
We will evaluate from each other,
In order to right Man's wrongs,
To vanquish and overcome our weaknesses forever.

Patricia Rose Thompson

Angels

God sends his special angels
When I am in times of pain
To comfort and to cheer me up
To stop me when I start to complain
And when I think life has no worth
And all my friends are gone
God's angels appear out of the blue
To show me I can go on
One was there for me today
Waiting with ready smile
Another stopped me in the street
And bade me chat a while
Each time I am upset and lost
The angels make me laugh
After I have met with them
I don't feel bad by half
We sometimes need reassurance
When life seems hard to bear
These angels are God's people on Earth
To remind us He is always there
Although He is not here in person
These angels do carry His name
They look like ordinary people
And are dressed up just the same
With them I feel a whole lot happier
That God is watching overhead
And now I can feel His presence
Pain is not something I dread

Michelle Clancy

In The Quiet Of The Day

Sitting, in the quiet of the day
Thinking of the way . . .
Suffering as we often do
Wondering -
If only we knew.

Time, it passes, so slow
Watching -
Waiting, for a plan
Knowing, surely we are not alone.

We cannot hear,
We cannot see
The plans ahead God has
For you, for me.

Waiting patiently for a sign
An open door, to which we're blind.
Sometimes the door opens wide
To which we see
Ahead for you, for me.

A road, a path
We must not stray
Seeing clearly
At the close of day.

Val Connolly

Colour Your World

'Paint' your week in colour to make the days seem brighter
Then every chore you have to do is bound to feel much lighter
Though Monday can be rather dull, when the linen basket is very full
The washing and ironing can cause a frown
And if it's raining this day feels 'brown'
But don't let it bother you, it'll soon be alright
All you have to do is 'paint' it white

Dress up on Tuesday, get away from the sink
Go out and enjoy yourself, you'll soon feel in the pink
On Wednesday, tidy up and clean
Then do the gardening and the day will seem green
When the work is all done and you feel quite mellow
Then Thursday, I feel, is definitely yellow.

On Friday there's the shopping, so get up and go
And 'paint' the day blue or indigo
On Saturday when the family is home
And the house is so much fuller
And filled with lots of love and warmth
Then orange is this one's colour

On Sunday stay a bit longer in bed
Make this day decidedly red
Enjoy a day of golden leisure
Which ends a colourful week of work and pleasure

Jean M Wood

Triumph House - Spiritual Reflections 2007

Your Warmth

Let the warmth of your heart be your barometer
And inner prompting steer your chart
Let the wind in your hair be your weathervane
And the sea be where you start!

Let the poise in your person stay your course
And joy billow forth your sail
Let the storms be greeted by your calm
And good tidings, these gifts prevail!

Let your conscience be your star guide
And your passage onward press
Let goodwill be your stowage
And love be your quest!

Let stalwart courage be your anchor
And angelic spirits your ship surround
Let Heaven be your journey
And the prize will be a crown!

Let the beat of your heart be your psychometer
And inner light guide your way
Let the beauty of your life be your landscape
And wisdom your soul's array!

Heather Ingrid Greenwald

World Vision

Everything is there for us to grasp
Extend your hand to God and ask
To guide us through the world and see
The beauty over land and sea

We are here to play a part
God's creations from the very start
The stage is set to play our duty
To live in this huge world of beauty

We must look around and be aware
How much there is - and really care
As only one life here which quickly goes
Like a vision bright and then repose

The moon, the stars far up above
Shining down for us to love
The beauty of the oceans blue
All part of this huge world review

Our future here is not forever
But God has plans, He will endeavour
To take us to a better land
And gently guide us by His hand

W Gibb

Role Reversal

I have peeled, revealed the layers
to identify your needs,
denial makes this task so hard,
the source on which your spirit feeds.

Your independence lies in shreds,
intruders threaten lifelong pride.
I see the panic in your eyes,
a helplessness you fight to hide.

Now you are old, your mind is still keen,
your body fails you while mine's strong,
when I was weak your strength upheld me,
now the balance is all wrong.

As you regress, so I progress,
I hold the upper hand,
the scales of life tip slowly,
a move thus far unplanned.

When I grow old and my turn comes,
I know this dress rehearsal
will help me try to understand
the pathos of the role reversal.

Angela R Davies

Beginning/End

Newborn dawn-break
fresh sea rising
glimmer, drifting
endlessly
fragmented moments
Man's mosaic
destined, inevitable
heavenly
aphorisms all-forgiven
platitudes of never-mind
monologues of in-the-past-now
reassessed and redefined
pocket memories
cupped from tearful
yesterdays of hours gone
gossamer and brittle-spoken
young is once
but darkness long

Jamie Caddick

My Window In The East

My small window in the east
I keep it open, day in, day out -
Wondering at the floodgate of light
Washing away the dark corners in my room.
I keep this window open, hoping for only a gentle touch,
Vibes from your world - if you send.

My window in the east I do not shut
I stand and wait and stare out at the stormy night
Soaked to the bone and
Waiting for you
Are you coming?
Doubt! I never do.
Do you know my address?
My small window in the east.

Santwana Chatterjee

A Special Place

When fear and pain are etched upon our face,
There is inside us all, a very special place.
A tiny corner of our soul reserved for Him alone,
It's where He comes to visit, when our mind begins to roam.
When all our hope has gone and we are feeling very low,
As fragile as a branch, that begins to break and bow,
Hold on to your faith and ask what's in your heart
And slowly you will realise, of you He's become a part.
That tiny corner of your soul begins to fill with hope,
And slowly and surely, you begin to cope.
Because He came to visit and listened to your plea,
You came into the light and you begin to see
And as the days unfold and the seasons come and go,
A memory in the distant past of when you felt so low,
But you will always know that He is there for you,
A very welcome friend who will help and guide you through.

Glenys Harris

Just Live

Live life to the full whatever your age.
You are your own person, the world is your stage.
You slip into this world -
A person to make a place,
To live your life, with enough space -
To create your own background,
Your life is a challenge, meet it head high.
Don't lose heart if trouble seems nigh.
Pause - look around, find some firm ground.
With renewed hope, you will cope -
With setbacks.
You'll gather strength, then go to any length
To beat them.
Go forward with a smile, as you travel each mile.

Doris Huff

Light

Go forward with the most genuine, most generous,
most brave part of you.
Let this part be a beacon of light pouring forth from your heart,
lighting your way, lighting up your face and eyes
with warmth, grace and understanding.
Let the guards fall away.
Stand tall in the fullness of the real you.
Do what you can, when you can.
Be open to openings.
Laugh with the fleeting winds of life.
Grow wise but stay young in your heart, stay light and willing to forgive,
ever open to learn more.
Ignore the cold guards that encrust the hearts of others and your own.
Remember that you can never make anyone love you,
you can only allow others to love you.
Some people love us more than we'll ever know but lack the ability
to express it.
Reach high but do not lose your peace,
never give up your soul for a false pretence of success.
Success can come to us in the simplest and unexpected ways.
No greatness was ever achieved without the innocence of enthusiasm.
And with your light, make your life nothing less than extraordinary.

Bridie Latona

Untitled

The rain pours down, relentless in its fall,
The world renewed by its vibrance,
I look outside and step into the fresh greenness and feel joy,
The grateful leaves and parched earth drink their fill,
Birds bathe happily, rustling their feathers,
The greyness an illusion
And nature rejoices once more.

Janet Rocher

I'll Help You Through Your Troubled Times

Hey now, chin up, there's no need to cry
Don't worry, mate, don't ask why
I know it is painful and traumatic, I know
But I want you to be positive and glow
Be happy your friends and family are looking out for you
Your neighbours and the whole world is too
Times will be hard, minutes will be trying
And if I hadn't known this, then I would be lying
I'm going to be there for you no matter what it costs
When you're feeling down at a remembered loved one lost
I'll be your shoulder to cry on every day and night
While I whisper in your ear that everything's going to be alright
Although the pain and suffering will hurt for a while
I'll tell you a joke that will guarantee your smile
Through all the gloom and doom there will be a ray of sunshine
                                                       and hope
And through myself, your friends, family and neighbours, I know
                                                 you're going to cope.

Mark Blake

Such Wonders To Behold

The wonder of the morning, as night clouds split apart,
The wonder of a mother's love,
It's there right from the start.
The beauty of a rose in bloom
Gives to all such sweet perfume,
The wonder of a baby's smile
Can cast a spell and us beguile.
The wonder of a starlit night
Can hold a heart and us delight.
The wonders this world gives to me
Such pleasures and they all are free.

Joan Winwood

A Ray Of Hope

(Dedicated to my loving nanna, Kathleen Norton)

No matter what disaster and what misfortune must overcome
I always see a ray of hope in the sun
As where we may not see luck, the sun shines hope
It always faces life to carry on by brightening each day
As this ball of fire always returns from clouds of grey
For it does not matter to the sun whether fear spreads the ground
It still returns in courage to shine golden rays around
Letting us know happiness still belongs to this world
Even though we may feel there is nothing left to spare
The sun is always optimistic when greeting us with warmth
Even if our paths lead us to despair
For it does not matter where the world's turning the sun is always there

It's when I see this ray of hope I wish everyone were the same
For them to keep on believing and hoping
And instead of giving in to be a part of the fight
By working together to find the light
We'll each hold a hand as a family, not alone
The world would carry on with bravery, together as a team
With hope and warmth to every home
Instead each stranger is neglected with every problem left unseen
I've seen no love shared from the people of our Earth
Nothing is heard it seems when people are hurt
Yet hope is there wherever you may find it
For me it is the wishful sun in the sky
That tells me to hope when everything has gone
Keep on shining and fighting for sadness to end
Then remember, act like the sun, carry on, carry on

Kimberley Otter

Christina Days

On days like these
I look around to see the music melody,
And suddenly I realise, it's inside of me

Summer sun and shouts from sons that only fathers answer
A hazy bell on the morning chorus calls out to her
Then sunshine flows like running streams,
And memories appear like Hollywood dreams.

On days like these we dreamed Ferrari dreams
Begin again trees sang day and night without seams,
Each second a hope, a hope in your eyes for me,
There's somewhere else I will be,
It's only up to me, and the thoughts of you I see

When your eyes awoke they danced with mine
Without touch I remember our flicks in time.
Our ages past each other's life-flow
But futures come, they don't go
Till then you swim in my oasis seas
I'd like to think I'll have some more days like these

Adrian Trowbridge

Wherever The Wind Blows

Like the dove of joy descending
Is the love of God unending,
And the peace You give, unbending.
Come, Holy Spirit, come.

Like the wind that blows unceasing,
Is Your power that keeps increasing,
And the strength You give unfleeting,
Come, Holy Spirit, come.

Holy Spirit, God transpiring,
Light Your light for us untiring,
Like You are, Lord, life inspiring,
Come, Holy Spirit, come.

G T Terry

Thinking

As I'm sitting on my bed,
Thoughts go whizzing around my head.
Thoughts of summer, and of spring,
Thoughts of any kind of thing.
Thoughts of friendships,
Thoughts of foes,
Thoughts about knees,
And thoughts about toes.
Thoughts about flowers,
So fresh in the rain.
Thoughts about France
And thoughts about Spain.
Thoughts about pizza,
All covered in cheese.
Thoughts about you and
Thoughts about me.
No thoughts about homework
(That hasn't been done).
I'll think of an island,
And I'll sit in the sun.
And thoughts about postcards
Saying 'Wish you were here'.
Fluffy pink candyfloss
Bought from the pier.
With thoughts of fresh apples
So crisp in my hand.
Mum's lemon meringue pudding,
The best in the land!
Thoughts about fashion
Or starting a trend.
But for now my thinking
Must come to an end.
It's time to store all my thoughts away
And continue thinking another day.

Helen Moll

Food Of Love?

'I don't want it,' she moodily says
As she pushes her plate away.
'I won't eat it,' she pitifully cries
And part of *me* crumples, and dies.

Every mealtime is a battleground,
She plays with food, pushing it around.
Images on posters, pictures on the news,
Fail to impress or change her views.

Do the poor suffer eating disorders?
Poverty and hunger cross war-torn borders.
My precious girl, so pale and so thin,
You must overcome your demons within.

I will support, go to any length,
To help you regain beauty and strength.
Ours is a journey troubled and long,
To re-educate, and make you strong.

Brenda Artingstall

Extremely Precious Day

Sophie jumps on the trampoline
She is almost three years old.
Her cousin Thomas joins her
He's a wee bit older and a tad more bold.

I can't climb up and on
So I watch them from the ground
And soon the others come and join
As babies frolic in the round.

On this lovely summer morn
I watch them romp, exuberant and gay
My children and their children all together
And I thank God for this extremely precious day.

Janet Scrivens

No Name/Her Words

No name is required
For she will recognise
Her words
No name is needed
For she will remember
Her words

Her words
That she read and cried
For she'd not seen
Or been told that
She had such beauty
Her words

Drawn, to the sound of her voice,
Its softly spoken tones, not so as to discern
The words or their detail, merely their fall in earshot.
I close my eyes and I'm drawn under windswept skies,
Over heathers and the hills, I comb the coastline's tidemark
And islands north from here - the homeland of her whispers.

For these words are hers
Long may they remain so
Long may she feel their warmth
These words are hers
And hers alone
You can look
You can read
But never disturb

R R Gould

Fear You Not

Do not be afraid
for you are mine.
You have been called by name,
I will not let you go.

Indeed, I know
how many times your trust in Man
has turned to dust.

Remember, I am God
and they are only men.

I know you are afraid of failing Me.
And it is true you are not perfect yet!
Nor will be
till I call you home.

As I have said down all the centuries,
believe in Me
and strive
to do as I did when alive
on Earth.

For then, beloved,
with My spirit in you
and My word to comfort
and to guide,
there is no need to be afraid.
It is not men you trust,
nor in yourself,
for I, your God, am at your side.
I'll not let you fail
if your desire and will
are there.
Just ask, and seek and find.

Diana Morcom

Dawning Of Life

Fascinating, incredible, beyond belief
To see our grandson's three-month scan,
Developing and evolving into life
As he grows within his mother womb.

Swirling in the soup of life
A new human being has been formed,
Attached to his mother's lifeline
Where every cell of life has to fight.

Darkness or light his eyes cannot see
Umbilical links so he can breathe.
Credulous though miniature in size
A living, created human being.

His growing is one of life's miracles
Complex and very unique,
He is as no other, not a copy,
But a gift of God's miracle dust.

To hold that scan photograph in my arms,
No longer a negative but a developed reality,
Unaware of his epic voyage, from microcosms,
Cells, to a healthy, bouncing baby boy.

Nine long months we had to wait,
To foster Heaven's poor little waif,
Fragile, his blue, wide, ocean eyes
Gave all that welcomed him an Irish smile.

He was born in the Whittington hospital
Near the archway road,
Weighing in at seven pounds, five ounces
On May the 30th 2006, at quarter past four.

Philip A McDonnell

Deep-Rooted

The beauty of the lilac - gone
With battering of wind upon
Each frail and tender bloom.
Day after day the onslaught came
From north and south, to make its claim,
To bend and twist and cause the pain
'Til low the blossoms strewn!

Life can be thus as cold winds blow
Upon our plans we make, to grow
Into our perfect plan.
As beauty made by human thought
Is suddenly destroyed. We're caught
In pain and bruising, to be taught
The empty ways of Man!

Far better to be in the sway
Of One who knows each twisting way,
Allowing Him the helm.
Then when the north and south winds blow
We can with confidence just go
To Him who will the answer know,
And seek a higher realm!

The tree remains though blossom gone,
It stands deep-rooted, firm and strong
To bloom another year.
We too can stand whate'er the strife
That comes upon this finite life
If rooted in the 'Lord of Life'
We stand and have no fear!

Elizabeth Bruce

He Cares

He carries our sorrows,
Our sufferings and cares.
He grants those tomorrows
While listening to prayers.
Attending to hardships
He calms every storm.
When cold and so helpless
He keeps our hearts warm.
Our great God of comfort
Dries every tear.
Filled with His faithfulness
Year after year!
How can we doubt Him,
As time passes by?
He shines as the rainbow
Through every dark sky.
Praise Him forever
For things He has done,
Ask Him in to make us
More like His son.

Elsie Horrocks

Precious Gems

Every single moment
Is a diamond from 'above',
So let us use them kindly
In giving all our love.

For in giving we are getting,
Tenfolds of love and joy,
What more could we be asking
For each dear girl and boy.

All human beings are precious,
And loved in a 'special way',
Animals love us always,
For they just 'look' and 'say'.

Eirlys Evans

Listen

Noise hems us in today on every hand.
The constant drone of traffic, engine's roar,
The hammer blows of strident band
Pulsating from the disco's floor.
All these assault and hurt the ear,
Distort, impair, stun, make immune,
Till softer sounds we cannot hear,
To nature's music out of tune.
Be still and listen, deep and long,
Relax and feel the sun and breeze,
Till, healed, you hear the blackbird's song,
The distant rustling of the trees.
Let mind and hearing reconnect,
Perceive the message through the word.
Don't shun your neighbour, recollect
She's lonely and longs to be heard,
Heed well that wise and gentle voice
That seeks to guide you when you pray.
Though worldly pleasures shout for choice
'I am the life, the truth, the way'.

V E Godfrey

Magpie!

Every morning I see you
All shining black and white,
With your long pointed black tail
Tapping behind you on the path.

I nod you, I salute you,
Upon your merry way,
With or without your partner,
Come what may.

I feel it is lucky to see you
All the time.
The black and white wonder
That shines.

A truly beautiful, wondrous sight
As you take flight:
Way up in the big blue sky
As free as free can be.
To where you will descend
On an unsuspecting tree!

Sara Jane Tucker

Lifeline

Knowing someone is there
Someone who cares
Makes life so easy
To help and to share

Someone to talk to
Is there someone there?
Talk to me, someone
Show me you care

Now I am happy
That I know you are there
I shall share, you my lifeline
I know now that you care

Mair Handley

Another Day

I wake up every morning
To the cock crow that is the
Harbinger of yet another day
With good feelings
The troubles of yesterday pale
And diminish with the freshness of
A new dawn
I feel the life force
Throbbing through my system
And I am reminded that
I am alive to face
Another day's toil
Each day is besieged by troubles -
Troubles that are mighty
Or insignificant as we imagine
Though life's troubles never
Takes leave I shall triumph
For they last a span
Though bedevilled by them
They spice our existence
For I cannot imagine life
Without a hitch to unsnag.

Emmanuel Ibu

Worry Not

Today is the tomorrow
You worried about yesterday
And all is well.
A problem you can't
Do anything about
Don't worry
If you can do something,
There is no worry
Faith will see you through.

Irene G Corbett

Reflections On The Alterations At Our Local Park

Our local park receives its transformation
With hedge and garden all stripped down.
Reverting to its first creation
Landscaped by Capability Brown.
The rose garden cleared of coloured sheen,
Its blooms have said their last adieu.
The beech hedge, turning to its summer green,
Torn out in haste to clear the interrupted view
From the great paladin mansion, now restored.
Its ancient splendour now revealed,
Cleaned, sand-blasted, pompadoured,
Its beauty, and its elegance, firmly sealed.
A ha-ha dug to replace the destroyed hedge,
To lose the need for fence or paling.
And so the eager people quickly dredge
The glorious view from ancient house unveiling
The shining reaches of the lake,
And lakeside trees in shimmering glory,
Then, travelling across the grasslands make
A new, and fast unfolding story.
They say that's what the park was like
When long-gone people saw its first arrival,
A jewel, a wonder sure to stir the psyche,
A worthwhile recreation, a most desired revival,
But is it so? Should we go back in time
To try and recreate an age that's past?
To needlessly destroy could be a crime.
Or should the future beckon with a really new re-cast?

Jack Scrafton

My Firstborn

'It's new and it's scary and it's OK because I know that you
                                          don't understand
Don't worry, you won't ever need to,' were the words I said as your
                                    little finger gripped my hand.
'I bet these noises overwhelm you and I bet all these lights do too
Well, welcome to this world, there are many of them but this one
                                          is special
Because this one belongs to me and you

And do you want to know a secret?' I confessed
'This all overwhelms me just as much
What is it you are thinking, what are these strange hands like to touch?
Words can't describe this, so I won't even try
Let's sit here, just you and me, and let the time pass by.

You know I didn't understand all this either until a moment ago
So much I took for granted, now it's clear, now for sure I know
All the things I thought important and worried about night after night
With a new sense of perspective, I see in a different light.

The demands and stresses that I thought important now take
                                    not even second place
Even the bad luck and hard times I lamented now fade with little trace
All that ever will be important, this one thing you must
                              always understand
Is the person who I hold here whose head sleeps soundly in my hand.'

Steve Prout

Only Love Will Prevail

To banish the darkness you turn on the light
an eye for an eye only deepens the night,
so turn the other cheek with all of your might
when stung by harsh words of venom and spite.

For revenge is the pathway of those who fail
to see past their heartache, pain and betrayal
to the lesson of Jesus through all His travail
that whatever may come, only love will prevail.

Think of His lesson when night calls at your door
with anger, injustice or lies galore,
try to refrain from settling the score
and bide with God's justice till night is no more.

Events may not turn out as well as they might,
you may look defeated in mortal Man's sight
but God looks within to your goodness and light,
so be of good courage and keep shining bright.

Susan Carr

Ode To A Friend

When my hurt was more
than I could bear -
and I closed my eyes
and refused to care -
you blessed me with your
wisdom, kindness and strength
and made me swim
when I wanted to sink.

That's why this comes
with so much love
in every word and line to say
thank you for being my friend
and helping me along the way.

Debra Ann Freeman

Morning Shadows

When night falls,
And breathes its scented shadow 'cross the land,
'Tis then I lay,
And turning thoughts within my mind,
Decide the outcome of the day.

Solutions sought
Pass slowly through the stillness of the night,
Then fly . . . !
Like morning shadows,
Rude-awakened by the light.

Sleep comes,
All conscious thought takes wing,
'Tween bouts of sleep;
Low-whispered words;
. . . and following;
Arrives the dawn,
. . . the herald's call,
To start another day,
I rise from peaceful slumber
. . . peaceful Heaven,
Where I lay.

Robert Tose

Just An Event

As the pain of frustration with tears began,
amok ran questions deep within.
Defeat became a known companion,
my desire for success a figment of imagination.
A word at length, heaven-sent,
'You can't relent, this is my intent'.
In life, failure is just an event,
you only get better with each attempt.

A Adekoya

Our Life

(For Alvin as we celebrate our ruby anniversary on 22.7.07)

If I could paint a memory
of a special time in my life
it would have to be the wonderful day
you took me for your wife.

If I could paint a memory
of the happy times we have shared
of kindness, love and laughter
and how much you have really cared.

If I could paint a memory
of the sorrows that have passed
when your words of wisdom comforted me
and my tears turned to joy very fast.

What a wonderful picture my memories would be
a lifetime of joy - you and me
forty years as man and wife
God bless you, my husband, for the rest of your life.

Christine Hardemon

Nature Wins Another Round

Looking up across the hill
The trees are leafless, dull and still,
Things will change another day.
Soon spring will be upon her way,
Creatures who have been asleep,
All the winter in the deep,
Will awake and start to roam,
Looking round to make a home,
Birds are busy building nests,
There really is no time to rest.
The flowers breaking through the ground,
Nature wins another round.

Betty Mason

He Sits At The Grand Piano

And lifts the lid that hides the beauty.
The pristine, clear clean white keys,
Had not been played for decades.
Closing his eyes - his ear guides
Him through the music.
Silently she sleeps;
Awakened by the glory,
She walks down the hallway -
Following the sweet sounds of the instrument
And its echoes against the walls.
As she looks at him through the glass door
He stops playing.
But the hands of his clock still brush against his face,
Engraving cracks into his skin.
And his external age attracts his internal youth
Like a flame attracts a moth.
Until she came and sat at the piano.
He slowly reaches for her warm, gentle hand.

Melissa Brabanski

In My Mind

What a gorgeous day
Finding wisps of clouds
Scattered around a cerulean sky

Sun an orb suspended in space
Warming a balmy morning
Happiest time of day

Loving every moment
Face turned towards the heavens
Smiling a smile contented me

Warm inside a memory day
Look at the greens, blues, reds and yellows
Brightest in this sun-kissed day

All now a memory

Carole A Cleverdon

My Day

Sunlight creeps through the curtains,
The birds are already awake,
I hear them tweet
As I get to my feet,
My day is about to break.

My cat is demanding his breakfast,
He's becoming more vocal each day.
He has milk to drink,
As I feed him, I think
Of a cup of tea on a tray.

I turn on my little radio
To hear the news of the day,
Some is good, some bad,
And some really sad,
But things may get better they say!

The day goes like any other
With the chores and the meals to do.
The weather is fine,
Washing blows on the line
And a blackbird is singing too.

Sunset reddens the rooftops,
Seagulls screech overhead,
I watch their flight
To their roost for the night
And I think, *it's time for bed.*

Shirley R Thomas

Smile!

Go on, I know you want to
just a little one
you're nearly there
please, pretty please
you know you want to share
think of your boss covered in fleas
or not having any hair
imagine him in shorts and his knobbly knees
or a drawing pin on his chair
the cleaner binning his car keys
or him stuck on the big dipper in a fair
putting pepper in his hanky to make him sneeze
or eating his lunch and leaving the pear
I know you're going to now
a quick smile
doesn't matter how
just every once in a while . . .

G Culshaw

What's The Use Of Worrying?

What's the use of worrying, for it never changed a thing?
It's far better to be positive and know of the joy it brings.
For though the rain clouds gather and all seems dark above,
Remember that underneath, you are in the arms of God's great love.
Love that's never-ending, love that's here to stay,
Arms of love that can uphold you, whatever comes your way.

Anna Powell

If Only

If only we were able to say
Words to take sadness away,
But no words can seem uncaring,
When on our sleeve our heart we're wearing,
I say this in my own way,
Feeling both frustration and dismay,
Sickness is like a burning missile,
Day or night brings an ongoing trial,
At times we need our comfort zone,
Or our own space to be alone,
We need our loved ones all around us,
We feel secure, they give us status,
Without Jehovah where would we be?
He comes to our rescue incessantly,
He knows our need before we speak,
Because in our hearts he dares to peep,
I yearn for the new world, I know you do too,
There Jehovah's purpose will refresh like dew,
Our shackles will fall, tears may fill our eyes,
We'll be smiling because we've received the prize.

B Jermyn

Back On Track

Keep telling yourself that all is well
And with God's love it will be.
Look to the future, plan hopes and dreams
Go forward with bravery and pride.
Be proud by how far and what you've achieved.
Take one day at a time, don't step out of line
By brooding on what you've been through.
Keep to positive thinking
Have lots of laughter, get out and about.
Take all the support you can
And before very long
The dark tunnel has gone
Your life is then back on track.

V Lloyd Berry

Hero Supreme

Everyone longs for a hero -
Someone to follow and look up to -
Today in the world they are many and varied -
These heroes of young and old.
But none can compare
With the One I have found,
The One all are longing for,
Who entered into our world and time
From His own eternity!
He came to set the captives free -
To heal the sick
And make the blind see -
To give us life in eternity
If we would follow Him!
Who is this world's Hero Supreme?
He is the Lord,
The Living One,
The First and the Last -
Our Lord Jesus Christ!

Christina Miller

Glad To Be Alive

Where there is need
Love will take heed,
Love will be there
When there's a problem to share,
Love will help to soften the blow,
Love can give us the courage to grow.
A kind word and a smile
Help to make life worthwhile,
So let's not be sad,
But be glad
To be alive.

Rachel E Joyce

Saint Swithin's Day

July 16th, St Swithin's Day
Is it going to rain or not
For forty days non-stop?

In courtyard, I can hear a child warbling
Runner beans, my neighbour is offering
The fresh roses are blooming
The blackbirds are singing
Butterflies are fluttering
In purple buddleia bush

In the blue azure of the sky
Come some menacing clouds
But with such beauty
Around us, who can deny
To be wonderfully happy?
My heart replenishes of tranquillity.

Who cares, after all
If it rains for forty days?
Clouds have a silver lining
Earth has some golden sparkles
The secret is to be happy
And also everybody else around
Happy as I am, in my heart, in my soul
If it rains or not . . .

Victorine Lejeune Stubbs

Unspoken Words

Words perfectly formed within your head,
they're left unspoken
but not unsaid -
I read your face.

Words perfectly formed within your mind,
it's so unkind
that they are trapped within,
and we without are left
with just a glimpse
of brilliance.

Words perfectly formed within your heart,
yours to impart
with a look, a smile, a frown, a touch -
they say so much.

Words perfectly formed within your soul,
free to flow on every breath,
breathe in, breathe out,
there can be no doubt
that words perfectly formed within your head
though left unspoken
are not unsaid.

Sarah Fuller

Cut The Cord

The river delights to lift us free
If only we had the courage to let go
Our true work in this voyage of life
Adventure and discovery, waters flow

Tumbled, smashed against the rocks
Bruised and battered each time we fall
The current drags us down, till we decide
To pick ourselves up and stand strong and tall

Weeds tangle our feet, clinging tightly
Life's crystal self going its own way
Not understanding resisting temptation
As we travel along the road each day

But if we cut the cord, let go and learn
Taking a breath, moving, opening the door
The current will lift us free from the bottom
And we can climb, bruised and hurt no more

Better to die with no regrets
Than saying I wish I had done
This and that with our lives, not sat back
Had a quiet life and never won

So stop listening to those that tell you
Don't let go, cling to the rock of life
Take your courage in your hands
Release the weeds that cause you strife

Be a creature, be ourselves,
Fly and float with the tides
Open your eyes, see the world
Through your crystal clear eyes

Glorianna Gee

Pleasurable Things

First sign o' snowdrops
Thrusting thro'
Frost-bound ground.
Bleating lambs in spring,
A welcome sound.
The smell of fresh-tilled earth,
By horse-drawn plough,
The bursting o' the buds
Upon the bough.

Lazy summer days
Beside the riverside.
Burning leaves in autumn time.
Rainbows,
Arching over darkened skies.
The innocence
Of a sleeping child,
And when day is done,
The setting of an evening sun.

The sound of tinkling bell
Above shop door,
Heralding
A treat in store.
Accompanied, or alone,
It's hard to beat
A cuppa tea, wae a buttered scone.

Jim McGinty

Be Thankful

Let's be glad we have each other
As this helps us through the day
The simple things are easiest
And can help in many ways
No tidal waves or earthquakes
Hurricanes or volcanoes too
Our country *has* its downside
But it's naturally safe for me and you
No tyrannical leaders
That rule with heavy hand
Democracy here really works
In our culturally varied land
With many different races
Each with their preferred faith
They mostly live their lives in peace
With an occasional 'fall from grace'
We still have seasonal weather
With our sun and snow and rain
And it gives us all a talking point
With the stranger on the train
We all mostly like to travel
To explore, walk about and roam
But wherever in the world I am
This will always be my home
There are always bad things happening
In the paper or TV news
There is always someone worse off than me
Has always been my point of view.

Chris Leith

The Infinite

You may see no point,
you may not even care.
You may think it's useless
or tragically unfair.

You may look in horror
at all the hurt and pain.
You may think it's chaos
and totally insane.

You may find no answer
just a niggling why.
But the truth is within
your soul will never lie.

For every kind of action
and every thoughtful deed
is like digging a hole
and planting a seed.

One that will grow
with every minute and hour
and eventually blossom
into a beautiful flower.

Then you will fly
on the wings of a dove.
It'll take you to the infinite
and the infinite is love.

Nick Card

Inner Reserves

We don't think we have it within us
Just as we don't think that disaster
Will ever impinge on our lives
But when faced with a challenge
We delve into
Our inner reserves
And discover
Hidden resources
We had no idea we had

We may
At first
Take tentative
Or faltering steps towards
Those reserves

We may surprise ourselves
And others along the way
But somehow humankind
Finds
The strength to rise to the challenge
And meet it head on

Nayyar Shabbir Ahmad

Windows

I'll always look,
to that space,
where I want to be.
Looking better on the other side,
I'll try and I'll be free.

I'll always look,
to that space,
the roses on the ground.
The raindrops cloud the view sometimes,
but clarity is found.

Gabrielle Conway (17)

Monk Ease

There are those who walk
in a maze of mirrors,
unable to see anything other than
as a reflection of themselves.

There are those who stand
in a maze of windows,
looking out at views of perfection,
perfect if only there was a way out.

Then there are those who have written
rule books on how to get out of the maze,
but because they have never sweated blood
will never seriously be read.

And there are those who sit
unseeing and unheard, so awed
by the concepts mirror, window, glass,
that their amazement shatters ours.

GDP

Tranquil Shores

Sitting on the white sand
looking out over the sea,
two herons sit proudly looking out to the land.
Yachts and boats all colours and free.
Reeds and bushes make little coves
of privacy with the waves,
swaying to and fro in little droves
bringing pretty shells and seaweed
for children to save.
The sun is warm, making patterns in the water.
Nothing could make the sparkling scene falter.
Bright blue skies and sunshine bloom.
'Move over,' say the children, 'give me more room.'

Marian Clark

A Portrait In The Sky . . . (Nature's Voice)

'A choir of snowdrops 'sing' Your praises,
after bursting through a snow-clad wooden glen,
to live again, and as they look up to the sky -
Your face is hidden from view, by the 'Eternal Veil' -

'A Portrait in the Sky'.

'A school of dolphins 'Rejoice' in Your name,
by performing acrobatic leaps in the air,
as they swim in the Atlantic, 'noses to the sun'
in an attempt to penetrate through the 'Barrier to You':

'A Portrait in the Sky'.

'A herd of elephants wander through the African savannah, at dusk,
with their trunks held up high, in unison, to 'Salute' You -
as they have made it through another day, protected from
                                    human predators,
leaving their footprints on this beautiful, dark continent,
as their ancestors have done and look upwards to 'Acknowledge
                                    You' -

'A Portrait in the Sky'.

'The American bald eagle hovers high up in the Colorado 'Rockies',
surveying the scene below with his eagle eyes,
as majestic mountain peaks unfold, one by one,
as he is the 'king of the skies' - but pays homage to a greater 'King' -
the 'Ever Present One - Most High'' -

'A Portrait in the Sky'.

'An exotic butterfly dances from bush to bush, wings in the breeze,
transformed, free from the 'cocoon' of its other life.
Even though it senses its lifespan in this new world is limited,
it dances 'gleefully' spiralling upwards,
attracted by the 'light' at the top of the rainforest,
reaching for the sky;
to catch a glimpse of the 'Master Creator' -

'Your Portrait in the Sky!'

Lisa S Marzi

Krysia

Her eyes are velvet green, she's a superstar
Her voice vibrates like an acoustic guitar
Her hair is August blonde, wild and free
She's divine, simply a good influence on me
She's like a lioness with a heart of gold
Sometimes her words are timid, sometimes bold
She arouses undying hot fires of passion in me.

May feathered angels bow and kiss your feet
Alone my life would be shadowed or incomplete
But as a lock fits a key, you lock with me
Like strong roots grow up an evergreen tree
Like the sun or rain our love comes naturally
Krysia, my perfumed lady, my unlimited true friend
Your loving laughter is music soothing my ears
You tell me honesty must triumph in the end
You tell me deceit breeds only from our fears.

Secrets we dare not keep, they niggle us when asleep
Krysia, you taught me what therapy is here for
If these head problems I create hurt my heart deep
I must defeat anger, that furious beast of war
Krysia, your love is stronger and brighter than day
Queen of mine royal, I will remain for you loyal
Believe me, our unique friendship be no child's play
Stay beautiful as you are, drive any doubt away.

John Flanagan

Life Can Be Fun

Life can be fun, if you let it,
And put aside all of your troubles.
So enjoy yourself for a bit,
Without getting into some fuddles.

So when you feel down in a pit,
To help you get over the muddles,
Keep happy in mind, do not quit,
But give and receive friendly cuddles.

With life's fast pace, we try to fit,
With all of our world's changing puzzles.
But try to slow down, just to sit,
Relax and forget workload tussles.

Try music or play a drum kit,
Try tap dancing and do some shuffles.
Try acting upon a stage lit,
Try all things, but stay out of scuffles.

Play a ball game, with bat and mitt,
Have fun with your family huddles.
Entertain and become a hit,
In the rain, enjoy jumping puddles.

Life can be fun, if you let it,
If only we can all find more time.
Enjoy yourself, unwind a bit,
I'll close now, as I've run out of rhyme.

D Ranson

Why?

We enter this world with nothing
Of this there is no doubt
No need to amass a fortune
We can't take anything out
There's only one thing certain
That we are born to die
That's the only truth we know
And all else is a lie
We enter the world and leave it
The time between is life
Do we enjoy it or destroy it
With hatred, wars and strife?
Do we learn to love each other
Or kill our fellow men?
Shall we ever learn the lesson
Or make the same mistakes again?
They say we fight for freedom
The eternal question - why?
Why fight at all when each of us
Is only born to die?
Whate'er we gain with fighting
Of this there is no doubt
We enter this world with nothing
And that's what we take out.

Lydia Barnett

The Stranger

I know you, I know your face.
We met before, not in this place.
Not on this Earth in mortal form,
but in the dark, alone, forlorn.
When all was lost and in despair,
you came to me, I met you there.

I know you, I know your face.
We met before, a time ago.
When I was in the depths of hell,
you gave me light, a hand to grasp,
to end the tears, to smile at last.

I know you, remember me?
I want to hug you, shake your hand,
try to make you understand
just how much you did for me.
Now standing here in mortal form,
never thought to see you again,
although a stranger you remain.

What brought you to my insanity
and made me well, and set me free?
You were there for me with your healing power,
when I stood alone in my darkest hours.

I know you, I know your face,
now standing in this normal place,
I stare at you, you glance at me,
clear you don't recall my face.
But you were there, in that awful place.

Maybe you are unaware of the powers
that took you there.
Of the gift that you possess, of the love
that gave me strength.
And so we pass and do not speak,
two strangers in a busy street.
But I know what you did for me
will last for all eternity.

Richard A F Hall

A Walk On The Wild Side

The country lanes are quiet and the sun is high
The perfume of the hawthorn blossom sweet as I pass by
Bluebells in profusion grow as far as eye can see
With wild rose and the honeysuckle to attract the bee

A farmer sows his seed in a field there
In the dark brown soil so carefully prepared
His prayer will be for summer sun to shine
So he will have abundant yields at harvest time

Little lambs are sporting in a field nearby
Overseen by mother's watchful eye
A thrush with chirpy voice says she knows best
As she encourages her fledglings from the nest

The chestnut tree stands dressed in 'candles' white
So stately and imposing in its height
And weeping willows overhang the stream
Their leaves a dappled pattern in the water cool and clean

The nesting rooks are cawing loud and clear
Protesting when some predator appears
And soft west winds around the trees will creep
To rock their tiny baby birds to sleep

These lovely things all tell us that it's spring
We see God's creative hand in everything

Doreen E Todd

Summer's Sleepy Shires

I long to dream my days away
In summer's sleepy shires.
The fragrant smell of sweet, fresh grass
Awakens lost desires
To dwell amidst sweet Nature's boughs;
To walk a leafy lane.
In Mother Nature's joys I will, one day,
Find peace of mind again.

In wonder do I gaze upon
This green and pleasant land
And peace, such as I've never known,
Walks with me, hand in hand.
Forgotten are all earthly ills;
My heart no longer tires;
For I've found Heaven, here on Earth,
In summer's sleepy shires.

Michael J Parsons

The Light Will Come

Some days I would sit and thoughts flood in,
Whatever I did I could not win.
I tried to keep busy to block it all out,
I felt that I was to blame, there was no doubt.
As it came to night-time, and I went to my bed
The sadness got worse as it filled up my head.
I lay awake silently crying,
I wished at that moment that I were dying.

Some years have passed since I felt that way.
I still feel sad on the occasional day.
They say that time is a healer,
I believe this is true.
Time could be that healer, the healer for you.
There may be times when the skies seem black,
Remember one day blue skies will be back.

Jean E Holmes

I Am Near

My ways you may not understand,
and think that I'm not close at hand,
but you must always be aware,
I am the shepherd, and I care
for all my flock, where'er they be,
so just reach out and call for Me,
and when dark days should prevail,
on wings of love, with *Me* you'll sail,
until once more joy you find,
for I am always close behind.

I shall hear if you call,
and hold you gently if you fall,
I will listen when you pray,
and I will take your fears away.
Trust in Me, My child,
I am near.

Jacqueline Claire Davies

My Definition Of Free

Freedom is fullness,
Wholeness inside.
A life lived in truth
With nothing to hide.
Love freely given
No matter the cost,
Risks freely taken -
No opportunity lost.
Free is waiting
For destiny's call.
A life lived in hope
Of the greatest gift of all.

Caty Rowan

Out Of The Darkness

The first step is always the hardest,
Take that step, my friend;
Climb up out of the darkness
And the pain will surely end.

The first step is always the hardest,
Reach up and take my hand;
Up where the sun is shining
Someone will understand.

The first step is always the hardest,
But then when you are strong,
The next step isn't quite so hard,
The journey not so long.

The first step is always the hardest,
Look up toward the light;
Keep your eyes on the brightness,
Walk away from the darkness and night.

The first step is always the hardest,
But you know, when the dark is gone,
Don't look back to the bad times,
Walk on, my friend, walk on!

Sylvia Pearson

For Good Friday

In our world of darkness
Christ will shine His light
In our world of suffering
Christ will heal the pain
In our world of hatred
Christ will pour His love
In our world of despair
Christ will bring new hope again.

Elizabeth Mary Caswell

Onward

What do we think of the future?
What are our hopes, plans and dreams?
So much depends on how old we are
And what happenings our lives have seen.

We all look back for perspective
Aware of choices made - right or wrong.
But that's all over and done with
And life carries us swiftly along.

As children we relied on our parents;
In adolescence felt vital and strong.
Aspiration and ambition, the drives in life
To find out just where we belong.

Responsibilities of adulthood,
Earning, bringing up families,
Doing what is expected of us -
Absorb our energies.

The goal reached! A happy retirement!
Where do we go from here?
Relax - enjoy God's waiting room,
Trust in His tender care.

Deryck Southgate

Heaven's Gate

Heaven's gate -
Sacred heart,
Ever-open door -
Full of grace and love,
And mercy,
Pouring out - for all who come
To the sacred heart -
Seeking a welcome
And consolation.
Alleluia to the sacred heart -
Heaven's gate.

E B M Wreede

Reality TV - Help Us!

Whilst watching news of war
A thought it came to me
In a world that seems is governed
By reality TV

Negotiation's absent
Because talking isn't done
Words replaced by bullets
From the barrel of a gun

But if people had some talks
Then peace may soon come through
And to allow these talks to happen
I've decided what to do

We'll round up all the leaders
Who wage war with one another
And put them in that famous house
That's used to film Big Brother

With TV cameras on them
For 24 hours a day
And no escaping possible
They'd have to find a way

If talks reach good conclusions
Let the public have a shout
And if the world is happy
We will let the leaders out

Stein Dunne

Lilac Time

Who can resist
The beautiful flowers
Which crown the brow of May;
The fragrance-kissed
Loveliness of lilac-scented hours?
A myriad tiny blossoms
Cluster
In bee-witched drowsiness;
Bright
With the lustre
Of evening sunlight,
Perfumed with dreams;
Burdened with memories
Of days long ago.
A quiet gentleness lingers;
The gathering glow
Of sunset gleams
In a caress of golden fingers
Upon each lovely spray.
A distant church bell peals;
The peace of twilight
Cradles every living thing;
Softly steals
From the heart of the lilac
The sweet warm breath of spring.

Shelagh Coles

Daily Incidentals

The dawning of each brand new day enables us to start anew,
Rejuvenate our hopes, to make amends, do good deeds
long overdue,
Take hold, be bold, be resolute,
No procrastinating, go march along life's route,
Some days are full of sorrow, try to lighten someone's load,
Should it be you that's sorrowful, count your blessings, they are
like gold,
Treasure the many incidents of your daily life,
A loving smile, a gentle touch, compassion, make these things rife,
Notice nature's blessings, a wondrous arched rainbow,
Twittering sounds of the birds as they busily flutter to and fro,
Flowers of a myriad hues, sun dew glistening on a spider's web,
Playful laughter of some children, waves as they rise and ebb,
Splendour of a sunset, resplendent mystery of a silvery moon,
Give thanks in quiet contemplation and oh, so very soon,
Your life, your thoughts, more lucent, your prayers and trust in God
a boon.

Marjorie Leyshon

Hope

Wearily I open my curtains to find winter sunshine streaming across
my face -
And there and then I delight to know that God is in this place.
The birds are happily chirping - spring bulbs showing me they
are awake -
And it makes me think that perhaps I have seen that very
last snowflake.

The winter seems to last so long - dark days, long days, so cold -
But the sunshine invading my being this morn is just so very bold.
So, now can I dare think that this brightness is here to stay -
And the dark days of winter are finally gone - and spring is on its way?

Kay Windsor

The Hour

The hour was gone - and so was she,
She wanted comfort and I gave none.
I thought my need was greater
And as I turned I saw the church door,
'Give of your all to those who despair' it said.
My need was no longer greater than hers - my guilt was.
To take her hand, to hug, to console,
How many minutes of my inner self would that have taken?
How many times in time to come would I long
For what she craved this day?
And who would walk away from me?
My lesson learned, I turned and with glistening eyes
Saw before me the hands of those entwined in love
And thought of his and mine before this day.
I thought again of she who needed me
And prayed that strength and joy would fill her heart
And therefore ease my pain -
And I saw the rainbow's arc I had not seen before -
And knew that she had made me strong - not I her.

Gwen

Enterprise 08.00

A text message beeps to awaken her from sleep
And even as her eyes open,
They shine like diamonds that appear in the folds of the waves,
Oh the road to her heart must be paved with gold.

I move to make a closer inspection
And in the window I admire her reflection
But from gazing into the distance, she catches my glance and smiles,
A smile that lights up her entire visage,
She lazily chews her gum and returns to staring into space
And twists and twirls her chestnut-brown curls,
Her beauty is no mirage

Because my phone rings and she is there at the other end.

Gerard Gough

A Proclaimed Lady

There is a crack in my lid,
'Twas always there.
We had gas as kids when teased.
I responded with cheek.
'Tease Peg' was the crack.
Bear with me now
I had to put a lid on things,
With practised patience gave
Dignity in the working place,
Where some proclaimed 'she's a lady'.

Now in company of great excitement,
I speak faster to get my say, or I
May lose my drift.
As the years are moving faster,
No job to lose,
Less fussy about the dignity,
Tease me now you'll get it back
As the crack in my lid is splitting wider.

Margaret Gleeson Spanos

Faith

Faith in any language is the
union of minds,
The union of people regardless
of skin colour, purse or place.
Bless those who have faith,
It sustains them in whatever
daily selections are theirs
alone to survive.
Bless those who do not have faith,
For they cannot yet know
what they are blinded by.
I cannot explain away my own joy,
The safety, the blessings
of sharing in faith . . .
While in another land foreign to me,
Yet safer - more loving.
Religion in its most honest
ancient nurturing.
'Peace be with you' - the
hands appearing . . .
'Peace be with you' - in any language.
I'm grateful for this life of faith.

Wilma G Paton

My Forever Friend

He's with me in the morning, all day, and through the night,
He sees my every teardrop, and wants to put things right,
He holds me up and gives me the strength to carry on,
And when my heart is heavy, He gives to me a song.

He knows my every trouble, and hears my every word,
He gives me unconditional love that I do not deserve,
He gives me life abundant, and covers me with grace,
He took my sins upon the Cross, each one was erased.

He takes His hand in mine, and holds on to me tight,
If I should fall, He sees it all, and makes everything alright,
When times I know not what to do, He calls me to His side,
He tells me to let go of self, my vanity and pride.

Where would I be without Him, my life would be a mess,
Now the past has gone, a new day has come, and I try to do my best,
So when your life seems hopeless, and you find it hard to smile,
Remember *Jesus* loves you, and take a little while
To seek His face and tell Him that your life has all gone wrong,
He'll turn your tears to laughter, and give you a brand new song.

The door is always open, make this your day of days,
Just call the name of Jesus, He'll help you change your ways,
There is not one He'll turn away, however big your sin,
Call to Him now, He's waiting, for you to let Him in.

Jackie Allingham

Just For You - My May Morning

Golden rays of the morning sun,
Bringing warmth and energy to everyone.
Healing thoughts I send to you each day
With 'get well wishes', I earnestly pray.

My morning spring garden, I'll share with you
Finding pretty yellow primroses, forget-me-nots too,
Masses of bluebells, both pink, white and blue,
All nature's miracles, an amazing hue!

A smooth green lawn, so peaceful and serene,
My little apple tree with white blossom is seen,
And high up above is a sunny blue sky,
Birds are singing and tweeting in trees nearby.

This is my wonderful May morning glory,
With a heavenly garden and a bright colourful story.
I'm inspired and relaxed as temperatures soar,
This is a day to remember, this year, for evermore.

Next door, colourful washing on a line I can see,
In the shaded bushes, my three cats sleep happily,
Growing in a corner, there is red rhubarb and mint so green,
These uplifting words are *just for you,* in my colourful garden scene.

Stella Bush-Payne

The Shed

Every man should have one
From the day that he gets wed
Whether garden or allotment
Every man should have a shed

A shed can be workshop
A refuge or a den
A place that one escapes to
That's only understood by men

When you go on holiday
And get your suntan in the Med
You can't beat coming home again
To the comfort of your shed

Now size it does not matter
Because sheds are all the same
You can't beat sitting in your shed
And listening to the rain

As I pass into history
And for years will have been dead
I won't be remembered for my poetry
But remembered for my shed

A place of peace and solitude
Where many a man has fled
In this world of chaos
I will always have my *shed*

Alan Dennis

Corner Cupboards

My corner cupboard.
Is filled with so much dross.
Bits and bobs
Not good for anything,
Packets of thoughtlessness,
Jars of justifications,
Boxes of omissions,
And bags of don't blame mes
Crammed to the corners
Spilling out
However hard I try to close the doors.
But,
God's corner cupboard
Is a treasure store,
Never empty,
Always replenished.
A door wide open,
Accessible and providential,
Overflowing with all that He has created,
Full of love and laughter
And promises unbroken.
A treasure store
For the sick and weary,
For the lost and lonely,
For the unloved and needy,
For the sad and sorrowing,
For all who enter His house
And sit at His table.
All are invited.

Anne P Munday

A Tranquil Path

I allowed my weary soles
to seek a tranquil path
on an early day,
to tread gently a calming byway
where sun stars sparkled
in the wake of narrowboats
from an idyll age,
their tillermen with time
to acknowledge my smile,
far from the rushing noise.

Senses awakened,
at last I could concentrate,
put engines in their place,
in the background of my mind,
and rest.

I harvested snowy down
from amongst dewy grass
and then sought to find
those who had left such gifts.

Rewarded soon,
I broke bread
with these creatures of peace,
and majesty
and gave thanks
as they healed my needy soul.

Jean Caldwell

River Of Life

You're the river of life,
That flows into me.
A river that others,
Can now truly see.

You're the river of life,
That helps us stay clean.
When You will wash us,
In the purity of Your stream.

You're the river of life,
As pure as can be.
You're the river of living,
That flows into me.

You're the river of life,
Forever so true.
A river that flows deep,
Into me and you.

A river so special,
That only God can be.
A river so gentle,
That it fills all of me.

Tracey Farthing

Life Goes On

When you compare what you've got
To what some wish that they had,
You aren't long in realising
That life just ain't that bad.

You can have a foul day at the office,
Then have no peace all evening long,
You can have someone taken away from you
And you don't think that you can go on.

But when you wake up the next morning
And it's dawned a brand new day,
You know that you have made it through -
You'll be stronger, come what may.

When it happens to be one of those days,
That the world can seem to crash and end,
Remember what will be, will be,
Then it's over, it's not perfect, but
Everything's all right again.

Lauren Robertson

Tomorrow

Look ever forward.
Look not back to bygone days.
Alert your mind for what the morrow may bring
and let not consciousness dwell on injustices of yesteryear.
Despise the passage of time and look, look ahead
with anticipation, expectation and eagerness
to greet the opportunities of tomorrow.
The past is gone, dead, left behind.
Free your mind from the confines of regret for past misfortune.
Open your heart to the joy of now
and know that what fate brings can be hewn to advantage.
Release your spirit from the shackles of yesterday
to soar into the free space of tomorrow.

Mike Wilson

The Butterfly's Garden

Its wings spread out,
the butterfly perches on its pedestal,
exhibiting robes of summer blush,
warm oranges and bleeding jewels of gilded eyes upon a
                                              powdered surface.
The iridescent light of morning's touch dissipates
and within a flutter, the amber-lacquered dust flashes from view,
revealing pinpoint toes that caressed the platform.

The butterfly rises
and glides through trees dripping with opaque lilac.
Snapdragons protrude their ruby jaws from rich borders,
while a willow flexes its tendrils against an ocean of sky.
Drifting mist sails with waltzing clouds scraped high above on the
                                              greenery ceiling.

This is the butterfly's garden,
to my privileged eyes.

Sigurd Ramans Harborough

Crimson Lakes

What are the mornings like in England?
Sing there birds soft hymns in the morning sun?
From afar their voices to me clearly command,
Fetters disband, your own find . . . run.

Sways there grass over sunlit hillsides,
Where soars the little finch in lonely flight;
And with wonderful wing the raining sadness outrides,
Collecting stray sunrays before night.

Rides there sunshine on unknown wings,
Traversing hills, and dales, and rivers run,
Or finds its way to unseen things,
To crimson lakes, and other fortunes none.

Allen Ontl

A Busy Morning

Nature woke up early one morning, she had a lot to do,
Flowers were pushing up their heads, she had to paint them blue,
On the way she saw some butterflies and brushed their wings
                                                    with gold,
In a stream she dropped some emeralds, well that's what I was told.

She looked above and saw the sun was just about to rise,
So she took her paints and gave the skies a wonderful surprise
And there it was, dressed for the day, in a cloak of blushing pink,
And in the distance a sleepy moon was just about to sink.

She took some green - her biggest pot and daubed it everywhere,
On bushes, trees and blades of grass, she didn't have a care.
Then just for fun she took some red and set a bush alight
And on a forest floor dropped blossom, painted brilliant white.

She cried with joy at the work she had done,
And the dew was formed from her tears,
Then she sprayed it with silver and the fairies lined up to dance
                                                    together in pairs.

Christine Storey

Fields Without Red Flowers

Poppies now grow in fields
Where a generation lost flowers red;
Where white stones, aged by wind and rain,
Stand still to watch and guard the dead.
Known to God, they've lain at peace
Since that fateful summer's dawn
When others gave them to eternity.
In peace, but alas not yet at rest,
For generations since have come to seek
An answer to their frightened quest -
To who they are, and why they've gone,
And how they can wake to greet the morn
And stay alive to watch the sun go down
On fields that have no flowers red.

David Radford

A Better World

A kindness shown or just a passing smile
Can brighten someone's day, if for a little while,
Be thoughtful as the years unfold,
To children and those growing old.

Think of the lonely, make time to befriend,
They will appreciate the time you spend,
An encouraging word, a simple deed,
Can help solve a problem when someone's in need.

Little kindnesses cannot be bought
Yet create pleasure, so spare a thought,
Show admiration for those not so strong,
Perhaps they may feel they don't belong.

Those are blessed that enjoy good health,
Not to compare with worldly wealth,
The bonus in life is helping and giving,
Adds to the pleasure, makes life worth living.

In life faith and hope is what we need,
If we are determined to succeed,
Time is short so make life worthwhile,
Show a kindness and wear a smile.

Greta Craigie

Love Is . . .

There's a gift, I feel sure we've all heard of before,
It's been with us since time first began.
Not one soul can flourish without it,
Not one child, one woman or man.

Some search for a key to unlock its power,
Whilst for others 'the door' may just open.
It's a feeling, a need, an emotion and more,
A good deed or a word softly spoken.

It's our greatest gift in this mortal life,
It sets our focus upon higher things.
It doesn't come wrapped like a parcel,
With satin bows or pretty strings.

It's the gift of love and it's borne of God,
No other gift can ever compare.
Love always overcomes any trial,
Love is the gift we all long to share.

Love never desires to bear malice,
Hold grudges or hurt others' feelings.
It won't settle for less than the very best,
For true love has no limits or ceilings.

Love may get hammered by life's mighty storms,
But true love bounces back and never dies.
Love doesn't need to keep scores from the past,
Love doesn't need to mislead or tell lies.

Love is God's beautiful gift to our world,
His heart, His way, sent by Him from above.
It's just what our world needs a huge dose of,
This world needs God . . . because God is love!

Kent Brooksbank

My Life That Went

How do I know my youth is spent
My get up and go got up and went
In spite of it I'm able to grin
When I think of where get up has been

Old age is golden I've heard said
Sometimes I wonder when I get in bed
Is my ear in a drawer and my teeth in a cup
My eyes on the table as I wake up

Going to sleep say to myself
Anything else to lay on the shelf
I'm happy to say as I close the door
Friends are the same perhaps even more

When young my slippers were red
Could kick my heels over my head
As I grew older my slippers were blue
And I could dance the whole night through

Now I'm old my slippers are black
And I walk to the shops and puff my way back
The reason my youth is spent
My get up and go got up and went

I don't mind I think with a grin
Of the places my get up has been
Now retired from life's competition
My day's gone with complete repetition

Now each morning dust off my wits
If I see a paper read the 'Obits'
If my name is missing I know I'm not dead
So have a coffee and go back to bed

Gladys Stephens

Serenity

Walk with me through this garden of serenity
Take a stroll through its measured paths
Feel the oneness with nature and your Creator
Fearless robin at your feet will abide
Singing loving songs right by your side
Quietness and solitude engross each caller to the shrine
Show dedication so diverse; so divine.
Love of these waters that nourish the earth
Keeping alive our song and our mirth
Take time out of your frantic world
To hear songbirds sing melodies of life and love
Measure the freedom of a thousand creatures
In this beautiful garden of paradise
Where beauty is seen and held in fragrant flowers and leafy trees
Perfumed blossoms hold their own 'midst a world of chaotic din.
Walk you through this garden of Eden
To be free from malice, hatred and sin
Discover the peace that radiates from within
Each heart, soul and being created to share in the glory of His domain
Soft sweet breezes soothe the senses
Bring that certain calm upon the troubled soul
Arise, be refreshed, rejuvenated, reborn
Celebrate serenity, celebrate new life
New morn.

A C Yap-Morris

If Ever

If ever you feel life's let you down . . . let me be your strength,
If ever you feel the need to breakdown . . . let me make your
heart content
If ever you feel you've lost your way . . . let me be your guide
If ever you feel you've gone astray . . . I will stop the tide
If ever you need any help . . . let me give you a hand
If ever you need to dig away . . . let me be your sand
If ever you need a sign for hope . . . let me be your star
If ever you need to be found . . . I will travel O so far
If ever you want a shoulder to lean on . . . let me always be there
If you ever want to call someone . . . let it be me, because I care
If ever you want to hear a laugh . . . let me make you smile
If ever you want to relive your life . . . I will make this journey worthwhile
If ever this . . .
If ever that . . .
If ever anything . . .
I hope that life treats you kind and gives you everything
If ever this . . .
If ever that . . .
If ever anything . . .
Let me be the one to make it right . . .
Let me be the one to help you through . . .
If ever you need anything . . .
Remember I will always be there for you

Anisa Butt

Granda

From non-existence
To my birth
To the woman I am today

Your love has been present
You have always been there
Touching my life in so many ways

Your support always invaluable
Your wisdom with me you've shared
When I asked questions you'd never shy from the truth

But now you're here no longer
How I miss the comfort of your warmth
No more retelling of stories from your youth

Your tomorrow that never will be
Will always be my yesterdays
And thinking of you they appear so much brighter

When in times of need
Simply thinking of you
Enables my heavy load to become that bit lighter

As time marches on
I look back to the times spent together
And how fondly you called me 'dearie'

I hope I did you proud
And that I was a good granddaughter to you
In the way you were a great granda to me

Elaine Donaldson

Take Time

Try not to rush the hours away
take time to stop and look
for the beauty of the day
to be stored in your secret nook

to separate in your mind
the noise you want to hear
a distant birdsong so sublime
to value forever dear

the smell of a special fragrance
from a beautiful bouquet
flowers in great abundance
the scent forever to stay

so vital to connect and feel
to touch, to stroke a pleasure
embrace one's love and friends with zeal
memories always to treasure

a preferred desired sensation
of enjoying one's favourite flavour
maybe a combination
of passion to taste and savour

so when you're feeling very stressed
think of those special times
thanking God that you were blessed
with five senses to help unwind

Dawn Bennie

Aim For Perfection

Be perfect therefore
as your Heavenly Father
is perfect.

Perfect is a doing word
and that's the word of God.
Go do no harm, do good
that's the word of God.

God is love and in His Son
our Saviour Jesus Christ
God did all and all we need
to save us from our sins.

Love and God
Yes love my Son
He died to pay the price
And rose again to set us free
To love Him, yes, my Son.

For love is life
And God is love
To free us from our sins
He gave His Son,
His only Son
And Jesus is his name.

Who are you
My friend, my son, sister
Jesus
Our God, amen.

Almighty is mine, amen,
Aim for perfection God, amen.

B Pail

Thirty-One

Thirty-one
Thirty-one
Oh why?
Thirty-one
Thirty-one
So little time.

Thirty-one
Thirty-one
Oh why?
Thirty-one
Thirty-one
What a crime.

Thirty-one
Thirty-one
Oh why?
Thirty-one
Thirty-one
Give me one last smile.

Thirty-one
Thirty-one
Oh why?
Thirty-one
Thirty-one
To last me a long while.

Garry Bedford

Untitled

Creator, of every existence
When everything exists in You
How can You see me?
So small - so very weak
So helpless

I could never comprehend, just what You are
Never see, the majesty
I just don't understand why You want me

To think, You would rather die than live without me
How can I mean that much to You?
I just don't deserve You
Why can't You see?

There is no logic, no rhyme or reason
Perfect love, to give everything You could
So that I would be untouchable
So that I might have understood

In my weakness, in my frailty
In my mortal, human state
I can just begin to see Your meaning
It's becoming clear to me

On your Cross, You yelled to me
'This is love, and this is why
I want to know You, want to show You
For You, my child, I'll die'

I am nothing without You
Blank, empty, void
I have worth because You love me
And where love is, will never be destroyed

Now I know why You are God
And mountains move by Your call
Because God is love
And love is the most powerful of all

Lesley Tuck

A Spinning Fat Lady

A fat lady spins on a bike.
Her white teeth sparkle under the sun.
'Hello!'
Her smile ever so pleasant, greeting her fellow man,
Strangers and familiars, no discrimination in her voice.
A fat lady spins and spins through West London.
The sun, the wind, spin with her.

On busy streets, numerous eyes meet in silence,
Not a single word exchanged.
'Hello!'
A fat lady stirs a warm wind,
Surprised looks on people's faces;
Eyes meet in silence still;
Strangers smile as they pass each other.
A fat lady spins in their heart,
A moment, yet they noticed each other.

Yoko Hand

Raining Ambience

Raindrops are falling on my head.
The sharp walls closing in
with every shot -
pitter-patter all day long.
The grey air
bitters the bland blue burdens
of the masses
trudging along with their busy 'lives'.

On a rainy day . . .
the city has no beat today,
though I just feel
like snapping my fingers
and watching the lights on again,
so I can breathe again,
and dance with a glorious rainbow.

Adam Moscoe

God's Glory In Created Things

God's presence is in all things He created,
We might describe it all as God-elated,
The distant galaxies sing of our Lord,
His presence in them, ever underscored,
By glory and by beauty to the heights,
As when we marvel at a night of stars,
At the infinitude of cosmic lights,
Upon the dull red ambience of Mars,
While Venus shines in silver brilliance,
And distant stars in their transilience.

The hedgerows murmur of the ancient wonder,
As when a chrysalis is torn asunder,
And a fluttering beauty then emerges,
On silent wings and confidently surges,
Across the meadow, garden, field and grange,
While humble bees have ways of scouting sources,
How wondrous is our God; the interchange,
Of bringing bees to flowers shows the resources,
Of nature and the God who is behind it,
And marvellous the way He has refined it.

God was in Christ before the worlds began,
This Son of God became the Son of Man,
Who perished on the Cross to save our race,
And took upon Himself the world's disgrace,
And then was buried in a borrowed tomb,
But from its depths He thundered forth alive,
With glorious light for all the cosmic gloom,
Christ Jesus put our souls in overdrive,
To speed us to the heaven where He dwells,
As our Lord in nature clearly tells:

God in the mist of the twilight,
God in the circling foam,
God in the deeps of glory,
Allfather, lead me home.

Derek Sones

The Church

Our prayer

Father, help us this coming day
To find Your life, Your truth, Your way,
To share with others, from above,
Your healing grace, Your tender love.

Father, give us an open mind,
A will in other folks to find
The essence of Your presence there
And ways, with them, Your grace to share.

Father, give us an open heart
That each new day can really start
To seek and do Your perfect will
With grace, another life to fill.

Father, give unto us the grace
To give to others pride of place
As in humility we bring
The presence of the 'Servant King'.

Father, give us the Jesus love
And Spirit's presence from above,
That in our lives, and in this place,
We're channels of Your healing grace.

Father, in life, help us to find
That openness in heart and mind
That others in our lives may see
A presence leading them to Thee.

Laurence D Cooper

Drink To Drive

You told me not to do it, Mum,
I listened to what you said,
So, why did I drink and drive?
I should've listened instead.

I thought I was cool,
While I was driving through town,
So why did it take me so long,
To see I looked like such a clown?

The next thing I heard was *bang!*
I shot up the kerb,
As my front wheel spun round,
It was all a real blur.

The sky went dark,
I felt so ashamed,
I hit that young kid,
That could not be named.

He lay in hospital,
That following day,
He couldn't speak,
I had nothing to say.

I woke up this morning,
I crawled out of bed,
The phone rang, I answered it,
The young boy was left for dead.

Jodie Harris (12)

It's Good To Know

I believe there is no death
of this I have been taught.
I must admit it's far removed
from what I always thought.

It's good to know that when we die
we wake up once again.
Free from the miseries of this life,
and also free from pain.

Those people who we all have lost,
we thought we'd see no more,
I know now, that we'll meet again,
they've just gone on before.

It's good to know they're by our side,
they know our every need.
And walk with us through our life,
it's wonderful indeed.

Ted Brookes

Silence Aids The Soul

Enfold me in Your arms, dear Lord
Place my head upon Your breast
Where the gentle beating of Your heart
Shall help my soul find rest.

Day after day my soul searches
For the peace it so deserves
Grasping little moments of silence
In order that peace to preserve.

The precious gift of silence
Oft-times it does get lost
In a world of noise and confusion
Thou my soul dost know the cost.

Mary Thompson

27th May 2006

Mum,
The hardest thing I did today
Was watch, helpless, as you slipped away.

You fought so bravely all day long,
You tried so hard, you were so strong.

Although you knew the end was near,
Not once, today, did you show fear.

And then, tonight, you slipped away,
At the end of a hard-fought, well-lived day.

I prayed to the Lord to keep
You as you lay asleep
And that He your soul would take
Till came the time for all to wake.

She's gone,
And there's an empty space
Where once
There was a smiling face.

You had strength and courage in abundance,
Love unlimited.
You will always walk beside me,
A mother and a friend.

Ann

Dreams

I had a lovely dream last night
Of far-off places, warm and bright.
And in that dream, so silently
Upon that wave-swept shore.
I felt your breath upon my cheek
But then you were no more.

Another dream came swiftly by,
You kissed my cheek, I felt you sigh
As pressed your body close to me,
Those cheeks inflamed with joy.
Then gently fingered locks of hair,
In dreams you are not coy.

On you, the stars a necklace form,
To calm the breast's cyclonic storm.
The glorious moon, that fount of light
Brought sparkle to your eyes.
I felt your fullness in my arms
But lost you at sunrise.

Owen B Duxbury

Worship Now!

Crucified -
That's how Jesus died
But now He is alive
Eternally.

Like the Milky Way
His splendour is displayed
And on that appointed day
We'll see Him in his glory.

Come -
Worship at His throne
Enter in alone
Praising Him.

Like the radiance of the sun
God's precious only Son
Will return for His One's
Riding out in victory.

Awake!
Christ's slumbering bride
Clothe yourself inside.
Glorying.

Ruth M Ellett

Music

Music flows swiftly and smoothly,
Up the street,
Made up of thousands of tiny particles,
All of which are full of energy.

She swims in the sea,
Gliding through the water,
Waves splash,
As sound passes through the ocean.

She talks to us,
Like she's known us for years,
All joyful and soft,
With sound as her voice.

Without her we'd be lost,
In a world without song and dance,
Music helps us all the time,
She turns our lives around!

Rebecca Day (11)

To Two Cousins

Sidra Anjali and Rhoan Akash
Lovely children and so lovingly named!
I pray for you and for your parents too.
One day, I know, you will be justly famed.

Believe me when I tell you what I know:
It is most wonderful to be alive.
And though at times things might not go your way,
Try! Try! You will survive and you will thrive.

Every single moment is there for you.
The birds, the stars, the trees, the breeze, the sea,
Are miracles before your very eyes.
They are for you, your parents and for me.

People often say that the world is bad.
But after having lived for many years
I do believe that good will always win.
And so, my dears, work well and have no fears.

Reginald Massey

Triumph House Information

We hope you have enjoyed reading this book - and that you will continue to enjoy it in the coming years.

If you like reading and writing poetry drop us a line, or give us a call, and we'll send you a free information pack.

Alternatively if you would like to order further copies of this book or any of our other titles, then please give us a call or log onto our website at www.forwardpress.co.uk

**Triumph House Information
Remus House
Coltsfoot Drive
Peterborough
PE2 9JX**

(01733) 898102